BEACON IN THE WEST

BEACON IN THE WEST

A Hundred Years of the Stornoway Trust

ROGER HUTCHINSON

ORIGIN

First published in 2023 by
Origin, an imprint of
Birlinn Limited
West Newington House
10 Newington Road
Edinburgh
EH9 1QS

www.birlinn.co.uk

Copyright © Roger Hutchinson 2023

The right of Roger Hutchinson to be identified as
Author of this work has been asserted by him in accordance
with the Copyright, Designs and Patents Act 1988.

All rights reserved. No part of this publication may be reproduced,
stored or transmitted in any form without the express written
permission of the publisher.

ISBN: 978 1 83983 050 1

British Library Cataloguing-in-Publication Data
A catalogue record for this book is available from the British Library

Typeset by Initial Typesetting Services, Edinburgh

Papers used by Birlinn are from well-managed forests and other
responsible sources

Printed and bound by Clays Ltd, Elcograf S.p.A.

Contents

	Map	vi
1	Leaving Lewis	1
2	The Biggest Offshore British Island	4
3	Prohibition and Population	19
4	Crofts Fit for Heroes	33
5	The First in the Field	50
6	Aviators, Golfers and Crofters	62
7	Not a Land Problem, But a Housing One	85
8	A New Party and a New Council	103
9	The Yukon Comes to Lewis	122
10	Blowing in the Wind	138
11	A Quiet Revolution in the Western Isles	159
	Appendices	171
	Bibliography	193
	Index	195

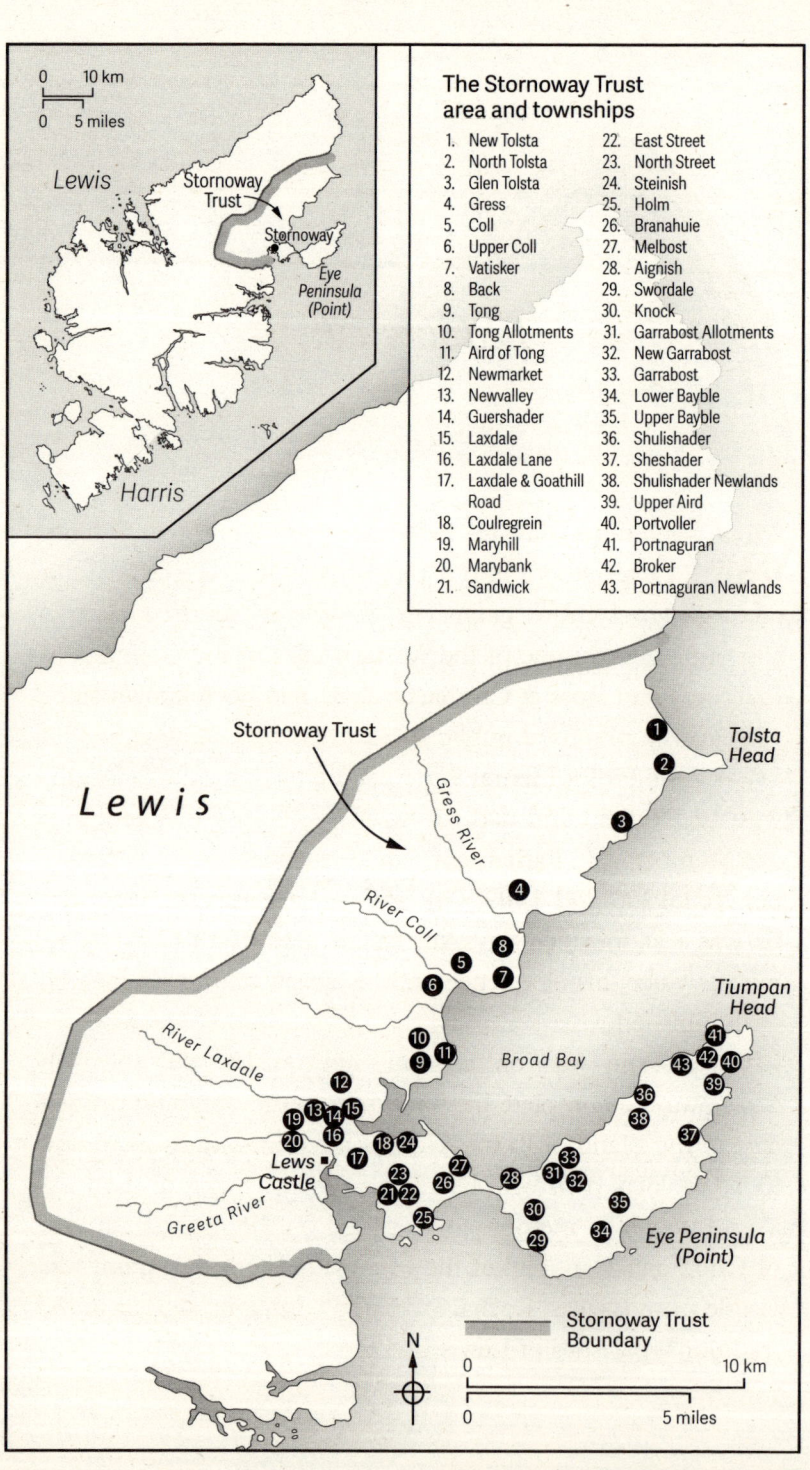

1

Leaving Lewis

On a September day in 1924, the trim figure of William Hesketh Lever stood atop a rise in the Outer Hebrides and addressed a sombre gathering of several hundred people. Viscount Leverhulme of the Western Isles in the Counties of Inverness and Ross & Cromarty, as he had been known since 1922, was a practised public speaker. He had campaigned on five occasions as a Liberal Party candidate in his native north-west of England and had served in the House of Commons as Member of Parliament for Ormskirk in Lancashire between 1906 and 1909. On that afternoon in the Hebrides he was just fourteen days shy of his seventy-third birthday, but his voice, his eloquence and his verbal stamina appeared undiminished.

Leverhulme was on a small hill outside the town of Stornoway to complete his final duty as the outgoing proprietor of the island of Lewis. He was inaugurating its memorial to 1,151 local men who had fallen while serving in the First World War. The memorial was raised on the modest summit of Cnoc nan Uan, Hill of the Lambs, because that point was visible from Barvas, Lochs, Stornoway and Uig: all four of the traditional parishes of Lewis.

They had enlisted from all corners of Lewis, and many of their surviving comrades were also present on the memorial mound in September 1924. 'In the first week of the War going through the whole of the Western Isles,' their Member of Parliament Dr Donald Murray had told the House of Commons in 1918, '... and especially through the Island of Lewis, you could hardly find a man capable of bearing arms. Every man, I should say, between nineteen and forty-one or forty-two was either in the Army or the Navy fighting on land or sea.

'We have had from the beginning of the War the long shadow cast by the setting sun of many a young life, darkening many a home in Lewis and the Western Isles. These sacrifices have continued throughout the War . . .'

As their proprietor, Viscount Leverhulme had issues with at least some of the returned soldiers and sailors. He had accused them of hunger for land, which they had expressed in night-time raids to stake out small plots and house sites, of subverting his grandiose plans to reshape and reinvigorate Lewis as a densely populated industrial island.

But by September 1924 that battle had been fought and lost, and Leverhulme had too much political sense to rekindle the fire. The servicemen were nonetheless on his mind and in his sight as he looked over the gathering and said, 'Lewis men love their home, their wife, their children with a passionate ardour that few can realise who have not lived in these wind- and storm-swept isles.'

Turning to address directly the young men in old uniforms, he continued, 'You have returned from the war demobilised but not demoralised. You and we all must live our lives bravely and worthily of the sacrifice the dead heroes have made and set ourselves to perform our task . . . Farewell, brave dead! . . .

With parting words we pray that your brave lives and noble deeds may forever endure fresh and fragrant in the memories and lives of all living and of countless generations yet unborn.'

His duty done, Viscount Leverhulme of the Western Isles accepted the thanks of the provost of Stornoway, Kenneth Mackenzie. 'Although I am not today as closely connected with Stornoway and Lewis as I was twelve months ago, my heart is in that Canadian Boat Song,' he said in reply. The 'Canadian Boat Song' to which he referred was an early nineteenth-century exile's lament whose anonymous authorship attracted perennial speculation. Its most celebrated quatrain runs:

> From the lone shieling of the misty island,
> Mountains divide us, and the waste of seas –
> Yet still the blood is strong, the heart is Highland,
> And we in dreams behold the Hebrides.

Leverhulme then departed Lewis for the last time. He left behind not so much a single 'lone shieling' as a baronial mansion overlooking Stornoway and 683 square miles of moorland and loch which contained a multitude of relatively busy shielings.

He also left behind the most significant and enduring benefaction ever gifted to a large Hebridean island. One hundred square miles of Lewis, containing the town of Stornoway, several busy crofting districts and almost half of the island's population would henceforth be owned, governed and managed not by the private landowners for whom the Scottish Highlands were infamous, and of which he had been a late example, but by a democratically elected local trust. It was a revolutionary gesture. Leverhulme had given the land to the people.

2

The Biggest Offshore British Island

The establishment of what would become known as 'community land ownership' in the Highlands and Islands of Scotland had been the last thing on Leverhulme's mind six years earlier.

In 1918 he bought the island of Lewis, which was then one single Hebridean estate. The 67-year-old multi-millionaire was in semi-retirement from Lever Brothers, the international business colossus which he had painstakingly assembled.

He had also been widowed for five years. His beloved wife, Elizabeth, had died in 1913, leaving this most devoted of husbands bereft. In the spring of 1874, the newlywed William Hesketh Lever and Elizabeth Ellen Hulme had taken a honeymoon cruise around the western and northern Scottish islands which allowed them a happy afternoon ashore in Stornoway. When, forty-three years later, he noticed an advertisement in *The Times* which announced that the 'sporting estate' of Lewis, complete with Lews Castle in Stornoway, was on the market, he will have remembered that land of lost content. He remembered everything.

He seems to have paid around £170,000 for the entire island of Lewis. It was a bargain basement price. The seller, a serving army officer named Lieutenant-Colonel Duncan

Matheson, was the latest of his family to inherit the estate since his grand-uncle, the Hong Kong opium magnate James Matheson, a son of Lairg on the Highland mainland, had bought it in 1844 from the Seaforth MacKenzies.

In 1844 James Matheson had paid £500,000. He promptly doubled his investment by raising the Victorian splendour of Lews Castle on the site of an old lodge, building utilities and curing plants in Stornoway, and creating shooting parks and private farms.

James Matheson cannot have anticipated that within sixty years the value of the estate of the island of Lewis would actually have fallen. He did not foresee the Crofters Holdings (Scotland) Act 1886, which was passed by William Gladstone's Liberal government in London and which, among other results, prevented Scottish landowners from clearing Hebrideans and other Highlanders by giving crofting tenants security of tenure at an independently adjudicated fair rent.

The 1886 Act tied the hands of Scottish landowners and therefore slashed the value of their estates. It also, as was its intention, confirmed the presence on their land of the Lewis people who, as Viscount Leverhulme would later acknowledge, 'love their home . . . with a passionate ardour that few can realise'.

On top of that, it massively increased the desirability of a croft and its secured crofting tenure to those same people. From 1886 onwards, crofts meant more than other small agricultural holdings. They represented stable footholds by entire communities on their precious land. 'These people in the Highlands are often looked upon as crofters and nothing else,' explained Donald Murray MP in his maiden parliamentary speech.

'[You should] look upon them as men who want to make a living. There is hardly an economic croft in the Western Isles on which from one year's end to another a family can depend for its living. The croft is only a part of the living, but it is a homestead on which they can fall back, and it gives them a sense of independence which working men in some large cities cannot possess.'

If the benefits of the 1886 Act, which had been introduced by his own political party, enabled Leverhulme to buy Lewis cheaply, the clear and present advantages offered by crofting tenure to residents would finally scupper his plans for the island.

Those plans were lavish. Viscount Leverhulme saw no reason why the island of Lewis, which in the 1920s had 28,000 residents, should not aspire to a similar population density as his home county of Lancashire and contain 200,000 people.

It was an interesting point to make. Lewis is a very large offshore island. Even without its southern adjunct of Harris, topographically Lewis is the third-biggest island in the entire archipelago of the British Isles. It is smaller than only the two main islands of Britain and Ireland. But in common with most other Scottish islands, Lewis had missed out on the British population boom of the nineteenth century. In 1821 there were roughly 12,000 people in Lewis. The ninth-biggest island, the Isle of Man in the Irish Sea, had 6,000 people in the same year.

One hundred years later in 1921, the population of Lewis had more than doubled to 28,000 – but that of Man had increased almost eightfold to 45,000. In the same century the Isle of Wight off the south coast of England, which has less than a quarter of the acreage of Lewis and is only the twelfth-biggest British island, jumped from 31,616 to 94,666 people.

In Hebridean terms Lewis had done well, for in the same period the populations of most other north-western islands fell. But compared to almost all inhabited islands south of the Scottish border, the third-biggest British landmass was lagging far behind. Leverhulme's mission was to correct that imbalance. His figure of 200,000 people was madly extravagant. In 1918 there were barely 200,000 people in the whole vast expanse of the mainland Scottish Highlands. But as a headline figure it would attract attention, and if his schemes reached fruition they would certainly demand a hugely increased population.

To sustain them at work, home and play, the new Lewis would be rebuilt and redeveloped from shore to shore. Its economy would be underpinned by fishing on an industrial level. Sea-going fleets of trawlers would set forth from modernised ports on every Lewis coast. Guided to the shoals by dedicated spotter planes, which would be modelled on First World War reconnaissance aircraft and fly in and out of local landing strips, the trawlers would harvest the fruits of the North Atlantic Ocean and carry their bounty home to be processed, packaged and canned by a huge workforce in Lewis itself.

The produce would then be exported to a chain of retail shops on every town and city parish in the United Kingdom. Those shops, which were usually independent high-street fishmongers bought up in the early 1920s by Leverhulme's people and rebranded as Mac Fisheries, became the residual remnants in the wider world of their founder's Hebridean adventure. The last Mac Fisheries outlet did not close its doors until 1979. The chain's half-century of active trading life was ultimately of no use to Lewis, but did serve as yet another tribute to William Hesketh Lever's keen eye for a marketing opportunity.

His plans for Lewis began with fish but did not end on the sea. Railways would be built to carry people and goods to and from all corners of the island, and even down to its smaller, adjacent neighbour, the island of Harris. Six hundred inland lochs would be stocked with such freshwater fish as trout, and beats would be rented to visiting anglers, who would eat, drink and sleep in newly built hotels.

Dairy farms, of which Lewis already had a handful, would be expanded and built to keep the busy multitudes in fresh milk. The empty moors and hillsides would be reclaimed and transformed into soft-fruit orchards, which would maintain a Lewis jam factory, and fields of herbs. 'Lewis,' Leverhulme told a guest in 1918, 'will become a great food-producing island.'

The plentiful seaweed on the shore would be processed into iodine and other chemicals. Lewis's prodigious reserves of peat would be mined and deployed at power stations to light and heat the island. Each year, 5 million spruce and fir trees would be planted on Lewis, to satisfy the burgeoning UK domestic market for wood. White willow would be introduced to meet the national demand for baskets.

The people would live in purpose-built terraced houses equipped with peat stoves. They would no longer require their old, thatched houses in the countryside, for in the new world they would no longer have their crofts. There was room in Leverhulme's vision for every manner of horticulture, but there was no room whatsoever for crofting communities. It was a hill that he was prepared to die on, and a hill on whose slopes his tattered dreams would finally perish.

In fact, Leverhulme began to row back from his grand prospectus almost as soon as it had been articulated. The export value of herring, which had been the main catch of the British commercial fishing fleet, collapsed after the end of the First World War in 1918, which presented an existential challenge to the established Stornoway drifters. In other areas of commerce,

Leverhulme might have been an old man in a hurry, but even he cannot have imagined that peat-fired power stations and fields of soft fruit, a railway network and vast spruce plantations would spring up overnight on the Lewis machair and moor.

As the complexity of his ambitions dawned on him, the proprietor was further niggled by intermittent land raids. The people of Lewis, especially the young men returned from the war, wanted not fewer crofts but more. They wanted crofts not only for enough land to keep a few sheep and a milking cow, but also because following the 1886 Act, crofting tenants had security of tenure. Once a croft had been allocated and a house built, its occupants and their descendants were there for eternity. After four years on the Western Front or the North Atlantic Ocean, that was the basic desire of the returned servicemen. Everything else, jobs in processing plants or on fishing boats or in forestry plantations, would be all very well, but they could wait until everybody's feet were safely beneath their own kitchen table. The wartime prime minister David Lloyd George had famously promised them 'homes fit for heroes'. They would settle for homes fit for Lewis crofters.

The Leòdhasaich were also far less interested in being the subjects of social engineering than were the inhabitants of the rancid Liverpool slums, who had willingly resettled in Leverhulme's model village in Birkenhead. Unlike the deracinated Merseysiders, the people of Lewis had something to lose in the form of an ancestral society, a familiar and beloved environment, a language and a culture. Unlike the new residents of Port Sunlight, they were the proud children of the third-largest landmass in the British Isles, and they would not easily relinquish their birthright.

They expressed it by raiding. When war broke out in August 1914, the Board of Agriculture had shelved longstanding plans to create new crofts in Lewis, particularly in the extensive, relatively fertile and crowded district of Back to the north of Stornoway. It was naturally assumed that following the Armistice of 1918 and the return of the servicemen, those proposals would be taken down again, dusted off and turned into reality.

They were not, because in 1914 nobody in the Scottish Office or the Board of Agriculture had anticipated the arrival in the north-west of one of the richest men in the world, brandishing more banknotes than anybody had ever seen and promising to transform the economy of the island of Lewis. The Board's crofting proposals were once again shuffled to the back of the shelf.

So the servicemen took matters into their own hands. As early as March 1919 dairy farms on good land in the district of Back were occupied and marked out for crofts. The group of recently demobilised servicemen who spearheaded raids at Tong, Gress and Coll wrote first to the Secretary of State for Scotland in Edinburgh and to David Lloyd George at 10 Downing Street, advising them 'that there isn't a landlord or even a Duke in the British Isles that will keep the land from us, that has been promised to us by the Premier and the Country at Large without bloodshed'.

They were irreconcilable. The servicemen could not understand why Leverhulme would not both create new crofts and launch new industries on the ample territory of Lewis. Leverhulme himself was unable to compromise and unwilling to have any small part of his vision or his authority denied. 'I had never met a man who was so obviously a megalomaniac and accustomed to having his own way,' said the Board of Agriculture's Colin MacDonald, a Highlander who met Leverhulme in Lewis on several occasions.

'Give me a period of ten years to develop my schemes,' Leverhulme told a crowd of 1,000 people in the Back district in 1919, 'and I venture to prophesy that long before then – in fact in the near future – so many people, young and old – will believe in them, that crofts will be going a-begging – and then if there are still some who prefer life on the land they can have two, three, four crofts apiece.'

They would not swallow such assurances. A young, returned serviceman named John MacLeod calmly told his new landlord at the same gathering, 'I would impress on you that we are not in opposition to your schemes of work; we only oppose you when you say you cannot give us the land, and on that point we will oppose you with all our strength . . .

'Lord Leverhulme – you have bought this island. But you have not bought us, and we refuse to be the bondslaves of any man. We want to live our own lives in our own way, poor in material things it may be, but at least it will be clear of the fear of the factory bell; it will be free and independent.'

Leverhulme was not given ten years. Neither the Liberal nor the Conservative governments which spanned his time in Lewis could or would, in those delicate post-war years, support the vaunting ambitions of a landowner before the modest aspirations of former soldiers and sailors.

The Scottish Secretary of State until late in 1922 was a Highland Liberal from Ross-shire named Robert Munro. Munro, the son of a Free Church manse, was on the right of his party but had a disdain for Leverhulme's fevered fantasies which in this case accorded with his party's political sympathies with crofters.

The island's Member of Parliament, Donald Murray, was another Liberal. Murray, a Stornoway doctor who had been the medical officer for Lewis, had called in his 1918 election address for 'a strong and effective scheme of land reform which would result in a speedy distribution of all the available land in the Highlands and Islands among the people'. In one of his earliest parliamentary interventions, in June 1919 Donald Murray called on Scottish Secretary Robert Munro to 'state when he will be in a position to introduce his proposals for the settlement of soldiers and sailors upon the land; and whether, in view of the unrest in Lewis and Harris, he will direct the Board of Agriculture to proceed at once'.

When he looked around, Leverhulme saw nothing but opposition to his proposals, particularly from representatives of his own political party. He would not relent, of course. He drew solace from the backing of a plurality of the hard-headed Stornoway business community. Opposition made him double down and embed himself in his bunker.

On their part, the politicians could do little but vainly attempt to strike a balance between encouraging Leverhulme's investments while also supporting the local demand for crofts. In the meantime, they held back from actually creating new crofts in Lewis, but pointedly and unusually refused to prosecute anybody in the island for illegal land raiding. In return, in 1921 Viscount Leverhulme, who was beset by other financial difficulties overseas, ceased to invest in Lewis.

The deadlock was suffocating. In April 1923 a tipping point was reached. An occurrence which was both symbolically and actually harmful to both causes, and to the future of Lewis itself, darkened Stornoway harbour. An ocean liner named the SS *Metagama*, which was then operated by the Canadian Pacific Steamship Company, sailed from Lewis to North America with 242 young Lewis men and eighteen Lewis women.

The *Metagama* was neither the first nor the last emigrant ship of the time. Perhaps 1,000 Lewis people went abroad in

1923 and 1924. She was, however, the most significant. Her passage in the spring of 1923 marked the end of an era.

Somebody had to give. In the end it was Viscount Leverhulme. Rather than compromise, he withdrew completely from the game and took his ball home.

On 3 September 1923 he called virtually every public representative in the island to a meeting at the Town Council Chambers in Stornoway. There he announced that he was to relinquish his ownership of the estate.

'I am now left without any object or motive for remaining here,' he explained. 'For me merely to come each year as an ordinary visitor to the castle, and knowing that I could take no interest in fishing or sport, would be meaningless. I am like Othello with my occupation gone, and I could only be like the ghost of Hamlet's father haunting the place as a shadow.'

But Lewis need not go back on the open market. Leverhulme would divide the island into two parts. Stornoway and its suburbs – which on that day he defined as everywhere within a 'seven-mile radius' of the town centre – would be offered wholesale to Stornoway Town Council. Everything else, the crofting districts from Ness in the north to Uig in the west and South Lochs towards the Harris border, was to become the property of the Lewis District Committee.

They were two distinctly different bodies in the potpourri of Hebridean local government. Until widespread local government reorganisation in 1975, Lewis was part of Ross-shire and was therefore administered by Ross & Cromarty County Council. All of the other Outer Hebrides to the south, including, counter-intuitively, Lewis's smaller Siamese twin of Harris, were part of Inverness-shire.

The county seat and local government headquarters of Lewis was therefore in the burgh of Dingwall, 100 miles and a long sea crossing away on the east coast of the mainland Highlands. As Lewis was almost half as large as the substantial county of Ross-shire, and Stornoway was actually twice the size of Dingwall, that arrangement was extraordinary. It was tempered by two devolved bodies.

Between 1889 and 1930, the Lewis District Committee, which was composed of the elected representatives from the rural Lewis parishes of Barvas, Lochs and Uig, administered on behalf of Ross & Cromarty Council such matters as public health, housing, roads, bridges and other public infrastructure in 'country' Lewis, which is to say, all of the island outside the town of Stornoway.

Following some agonised meetings in the September and October of 1923, Lewis District Committee rejected Viscount Leverhulme's offer. Most of its members wanted to accept it and take 'outlander' Lewis into public hands. But the sums did not add up; the books did not balance. Removed from cross-subsidy by the economic engine room of Stornoway, rural Lewis ran at a loss. 'For my own part I cannot see – although it is difficult and although it is disagreeable, and I would certainly like to be the first to accept the gift if I saw my way clear, but owing to this deficit, and not sure of what might take place, there's a certain amount of risk in it – I cannot personally see my way to accept,' said Alexander MacFarquhar of Dell.

After being refused financial support by the new Scottish Secretary of State, the rural councillors voted by six to three, with three abstentions, to tell Leverhulme that '[the Lewis District Committee] much regret that they cannot see their way to become the nucleus of the proposed Trust for the sphere lying beyond the radius of seven miles from the Post Office of Stornoway'. When the rural portion of the old Lewis estate could not attract one buyer, it was broken into its shooting and fishing lets at such places as Soval, Pairc, Barvas and Galson. The sitting tenants were given first option to buy outright their formerly rented playgrounds. A couple, at Carloway and at Galson, could still not be sold, and they were taken by purchasers from within Leverhulme's operation. A young Lancastrian named Edwin Aldred, who would play a large role in the early chapters of the story of the Stornoway Trust, found himself by such means to be the landowner of the newly formed Carloway estate.

Stornoway Town Council was a different matter altogether.

Like many another metropolitan capital, Stornoway had developed its own character and identity, semi-detached from outlander Lewis. The town had been a chartered royal burgh since 1607. In 1862 its modern Town Council was established, its elected members assuming responsibility for roads and pavements, lighting, cleansing, water and drainage, regulation of building, public health, public order, licensing and general amenities. Throw in a provost, two bailies and several magistrates, and early-twentieth-century Stornoway was not deficient in qualified and experienced public servants.

Stornoway Town Council was often indistinguishable from its business community. Its members therefore included some of the confidantes of Viscount Leverhulme and most committed supporters of his prospectus. It is unlikely that at least some town councillors were not consulted before the landowner made his parting offer.

Those men – and they were virtually all men – had made Stornoway into a proud and functional twentieth-century municipality. They were also more aware than most of the declining role of the island of Lewis within the United Kingdom, and of their responsibility to reassert their island.

They did not hang around. Their acceptance of the town's assets such as Lews Castle and its utilities such as the steam laundry and gasworks was never in serious doubt. Within a week the Council had met and agreed 'to accept the gift subject to the adjustment of details'. The adjustment of details would be substantial and important.

On 8 November 1923 Stornoway Town Council met to consider, and to approve, the draft deeds of property which would become the estate of the new, democratically accountable landlord of eastern Lewis which would be named the Stornoway Trust. They noted with satisfaction that Viscount Leverhulme's initial offer of everything within a 'seven-mile radius' of Stornoway post office had been radically amended. It was now improved to encompass all of the old parish of Stornoway.

'Within a seven-mile radius of Stornoway post office' proved to be negotiable. British post offices were frequently used as the terminal for roadside milestones, in part to tell the post chaise how far it had to travel. Leverhulme's legal people will have drawn up the papers with such precedence in mind. Stornoway post office was in the early 1920s situated in a tall and elegant building at the north side of Perceval Square, facing out into Cromwell Street. Sixty years later, in 1982, that former post office building would become the home of the Stornoway Trust.

The parish was traditionally a piece of land which reached far beyond the borders of the town. In the words of a late-Victorian *Statistical Account of Scotland*, Stornoway parish was:

> in the NE [north-east] of the island of Lewis. It is bounded E by the Minch, S by the parish of Lochs, SW by the parish of Uig, and NW by the parish of Barvas.

There is a compact main portion with a narrow peninsula running out eastward. The length of the mainland portion, from NNE at a point on the coast 9 miles S of the Butt of Lewis south-south-westward to the boundary with Lochs, is about 20 miles; and the extreme breadth is about 6 miles.

Some distance S of the centre of this at the town of Stornoway, an isthmus projects east-north-eastward between Broad Bay on the N, and Loch Stornoway on the S, for 3½ miles, and is at its narrowest point on the E only about 200 yards wide; and from this neck the Peninsula of Eye extends north-eastward almost parallel to the coast-line of the compact main portion of the parish for 7 miles with an average breadth of 2½ miles.

The total area [of Stornoway parish] is 67,651.862 acres, of which 2145.419 are water, and 2282.275 foreshore.

The revised estate map included the whole of Stornoway parish, and a portion of North Lochs which included both the Arnish and Manor Farm moorlands.

It contained all of the extensive district of Broad Bay, up to and including the township of Tolsta, which sat 13 miles north of Stornoway post office, as well as the whole of the busy and quasi-autonomous Point peninsula, whose furthest headland was over 11 miles from Stornoway town centre. The property extended even further inland, west to the Barvas hills and north to Muirneag.

Point was the *Statistical Account*'s 'Peninsula of Eye'. The word 'Eye' was an antique corruption of the Norse *Ui*, meaning a neck of land. The term was displaced by 'Point' during the twentieth century. The Gaelic-speaking people of the peninsula, who famously cared little for what others thought of them or called them, rarely referred to their home by any other name than An Rubha, The Peninsula, and to themselves as Rubhaich.

The Stornoway Trustees were looking at a property which included not only a busy and prosperous town, but also the fourteen Rubhaich villages – or 'townships', in crofting terms – of Melbost, Branahuie, Aignish, Knock, Swordale, Garrabost, Lower Bayble, Upper Bayble, Shulishader, Sheshader, Flesherin, Cnoc Amhlaigh, Portnaguran, Aird, Broker and Portvoller, and the further nine of Tong, Coll, Upper Coll, Vatisker, Gress, Back, North Tolsta, Glen Tolsta and New Tolsta on the machair greensward of Broad Bay, north of Stornoway.

As well as the coastal settlements, it included a large mouthful of Barvas Moor, the island's central feature which had for centuries offered summer grazing and shielings, and occasional haven to the hermit and the runaway. It had the 2,000 acres of freshwater lochs mentioned in the *Statistical Account*, some of which contained trout, such salmon rivers as the Gress, Laxdale and Creed, and peat bogs without which most Leòdhasaich would have had no heating or cooking fuel.

The estate finally ran to 68,000 acres, or 106 square miles. That was 15 per cent of the total land area of Lewis. It contained 10,000 people, or 35 per cent of the island's population of 28,000 inhabitants.

At a further meeting on 28 January 1924, Provost Kenneth Mackenzie told his fellow councillors that he had received the complete Deeds of Trust from Viscount Leverhulme's Edinburgh solicitors. The Stornoway Trust, the first and for several decades the only large community-owned estate in the United Kingdom, was almost up and running.

3

Prohibition and Population

The first task of the Stornoway Trust was to stabilise Lewis. As the voyage of the *Metagama* indicated, the most serious effect of the Leverhulme withdrawal was to create an almost existential uncertainty in that previously confident and assertive island.

Lewis in the 1920s was not a happy place. The Glaswegian physician Halliday Sutherland visited the island for the first time in 1923, shortly after Leverhulme's departure. 'When I reached Stornoway,' Sutherland recalled ten years later in his travelogue *Hebridean Journey*, 'I found a half-built factory on which work had been abandoned, a derelict small-gauge railway, and thousands of pounds' worth of machinery rusting on the shore.'

Halliday Sutherland was a recent convert to Roman Catholicism and he was equally distressed to discover that the windows of Stornoway's small and makeshift Catholic chapel had been smashed. 'During the previous year,' he recounted from second-hand information, 'a handful of Catholics had attempted to hold a service in the church and a crowd had pelted the building with stones.'

On top of that, Halliday Sutherland found it difficult to drown his distress. In November 1920, following the provisions of the Temperance (Scotland) Act 1913, the island of Lewis had voted for the prohibition of retail alcohol. In May of the following year, 1921, under the Temperance Act, four retail licences in the burgh of Stornoway lapsed and were not renewed. That local bylaw was agreed upon two years after Andrew Volstead's more famous National Prohibition Act had been enforced in all of the United States. It was not an unusual measure, at the time or later, in the Protestant Celtic fringes of the United Kingdom.

Across the whole of Scotland prohibition was limited. When people were free to debate and vote on the 1913 Act, following the Armistice of 1918, alcohol bans were introduced in Kilsyth, Kirkintilloch, Wick and Lerwick. At one point or another, sixteen council wards across Scotland went dry. But only twenty-three of Scotland's 253 districts voted for 'no licence' prohibition and a further thirty-five regions saw some limitations placed on alcohol sales.

Unlike the Volstead Act, prohibition in Lewis was necessarily an isolated affair. Not only did it take place within a country – within, indeed, a county – where the purchase and consumption of retailed alcohol was in other districts still legal and relatively unlimited, but its strictures in practice applied almost exclusively to Stornoway, as there were no public bars elsewhere in the island of Lewis.

It was a half-hearted and short-lived prohibition. It was certainly promoted by the dominant Free Churches, and widely supported by Lewis women of property who, having been granted limited national suffrage in 1918, found themselves suddenly enfranchised to vote in the local prohibition referendum two years later.

Bizarrely to outside eyes, it did not apply to Harris, which was still in the permissive embrace of Inverness rather than

Ross & Cromarty County Council, which had not held a prohibition referendum and whose single hotel bar therefore remained unaffected.

The measure emphatically did not, as Sutherland would discover, create a teetotal island of Lewis. In 1922, the first full year after the retail alcohol licence ban came into place, it was revealed that one Stornoway wholesaler alone imported ales and spirits to the value of £24,887, which was almost half the amount invested by all the town's wholesalers in 1920, the last full year before prohibition. Provost Kenneth Mackenzie, while paying lip service to the result of the local referendum, publicly regretted, 'The conditions under which liquor is now supplied and consumed are – to say the least of it – degrading and demoralising.'

'It was possible to buy whisky from a licensed grocer,' observed Halliday Sutherland, 'provided one bought half a gallon at a time. Men would club together to buy this amount and carry it down to the foreshore, where they drank it. Consequently, drunkenness was not unknown, and for the twelve months following the veto of local option, the amount of alcohol imported into the island had increased. In the more remote places private stills were working.'

Only smaller units of strong drink were banned. It remained legal, as Sutherland suggested, to buy wholesale quantities, such as cases of whisky and casks of beer. That loophole was intended to alleviate the suffering of large hotels, which were permitted to serve drinks with meals to guests, and to lubricate the social wheels of the bigger private houses. In practice it also gave a new lease of life to the rural township bothan in Lewis, to which Kenneth Mackenzie, whose roots were in rural Lochs, was referring as 'degrading and demoralising'.

In many communities a crude but largely weatherproof building was set aside as a drinking den. The men would contribute to a kitty, wholesale cases and casks would be – perfectly legally – imported, and the bothan would thereafter serve as a private club. This arrangement proved so congenial to the communitarian crofting townships (wholesale alcohol was, after all, cheaper by far than anything bought at a bar or even from a shop) that in some cases the shebeen long survived the repeal of prohibition and for decades staved off the introduction of licensed commercial premises.

In the rural district of Ness a working bothan survived as a viable alternative to a public bar for more than half a century after 1921, and it was finally put out of business not by a public house but by another community venture: a newly built social club run by and for the benefit of the local football team.

In some northern fishing ports, a full or partial alcohol prohibition held sway for decades. In the Caithness town of Wick, no public houses or licensed grocers were permitted to sell alcohol to the public between May 1922 and May 1947. In Lewis the ban on alcohol licences lasted for five years. It was repealed by another public vote in 1926.

In October 1923 the district Nursing Committee at Ness reformed itself into an Emergency Relief Committee. The headmaster of Lionel School grew so concerned by the malnourished condition of his pupils that he issued a public appeal for funds to provide them with a midday meal. Sir William Mitchell Cotts MP appealed unsuccessfully to the Scottish Secretary Lord Novar to resume the Ness–Tolsta road works which had been abandoned by Leverhulme.

Almost a full year of preternaturally wet weather resulted in the failure of the potato crop throughout the Hebrides and the west mainland. In Lewis itself only a handful of days in May,

June, July and August had been completely dry, just one day in September had seen no rain, and in the whole of October and November there was 'not recorded one single instance of twenty-four consecutive hours dry'. Peats and corn had been too wet to harvest properly. Cut hay lay blackening on the ground. Severe equinoctial storms blew down the few stooks of fodder and wiped out most surviving crops in west-coast districts such as Callanish.

The fishing industry remained in deep depression. Clothing and food parcels were distributed throughout the islands by charitable organisations and Highland societies. People said that matters had never been worse since the Hungry Forties of eighty years before. The fishing township of Cromore in Lochs was reported late in 1923 to be in a condition of 'destitution . . . there is no place, even in Lewis, where things could be worse'. A meeting at Back Free Church warned of 'starvation in many homes. The people have nothing to fall back upon owing to the failure of the fishing industry, the complete failure of the potato crop, and the lack of work of any kind.'

At Westminster in the new year of 1924 the freshly elected radical Liberal MP for the Western Isles, Alexander MacKenzie Livingstone, pleaded urgently but in vain for a Commission to be appointed to investigate 'the exceptional economic conditions prevailing in the Western Isles'.

The first Labour Scottish Secretary, William Adamson, who took office following the December 1923 General Election, acknowledged the 'exceptional distress in Lewis this winter' and announced that the government would be supplying the Highlands and Islands 'at a reduced cost [with] seed oats and seed potatoes for use this spring'.

Across the other Hebrides, land raiding resumed. In Lewis a generation continued to emigrate. On Saturday 26 April

1924, the Canadian Pacific Railways liner SS *Marloch* put into Stornoway and carried away with her to the New World 290 young Lewis men and women. Most of them travelled on the government of Ontario's Assisted Passages Scheme. The men were bonded to become farm labourers until they had repaid the debts of their passage; the women to be domestic servants.

Not all of the young men were gone forever. To some the *Metagama* and the *Marloch* offered an opportunity to adventure out in the world rather than settle on a Canadian prairie farm. Donald Campbell, the great-uncle of the memoirist, journalist and future member of the Stornoway Trust Calum 'Safety' Smith, left Lewis in 1926 and returned to Stornoway on the mail steamer in 1932. In his six years away, he travelled thousands of miles between Baltimore, New Orleans, Seattle, Vancouver, Winnipeg and Montreal. Following his return, he hardly left Lewis. Donald Campbell's story was far from commonplace, but it was not unknown.

Contrarily, the 17-year-old Mary Anne MacLeod left the Broad Bay village of Tong in 1929 for the United States, where she met and married the property developer Fred Trump. Mary Anne and Fred raised five children and in 1946 she christened her second son in authentic Hebridean fashion, Donald John Trump. She returned to Lewis on several occasions but died in the year 2000, still as a Leòdhasach Gaelic speaker in New York.

The population of Lewis haemorrhaged. In the course of the 1920s, for the first time in recorded history, the demographic size of the whole of Scotland fell. According to two national censuses, it was reduced from 4,888,407 in 1921 to 4,842,989 in 1931. That was a disturbing statistic which merited the attention it received. It was, however, a fall of less than 1 per cent, which was more than made up the next time a census was taken in 1951.

In contrast, the National Census of 1931 showed a Lewis population of 25,205. That represented a fall of 4,398 people from the pre-war headcount of 29,603, which had been registered in 1911. It was a population loss, in just two decades, of nearly 15 per cent.

Only part of that distressing percentage could be ascribed, directly or indirectly, to deaths in the Great War. Lewis had, as was evidenced on the memorial hill outside Stornoway in 1924, lost a disproportionately high number of young men between 1914 and 1918. The island's dead and missing in action were joined in the early hours of 1 January 1919 by the cataclysmic sinking of the troop-carrying steam yacht HMY *Iolaire*, which drowned a further 201 men, most of them from Lewis, on the outskirts of Stornoway harbour. The Hebrides also lost their share of people to the 'Spanish flu' pandemic of 1918 to 1920.

So between 1911 and 1921 the population of Lewis fell by 1,225 people, or 4 per cent.

In the post-war decade of 1921–31, however, almost three times that number went missing. In total, no fewer than 3,173 people, or 11 per cent of the Lewis population, disappeared in those ten peacetime years. The people who remained did not need to ask where most of them had gone. They had waved them off from Stornoway harbour on the *Metagama* and the *Marloch*. They had received their letters home from Ontario, New South Wales and Patagonia. This evaporation of people was taking place in an island whose last proprietor had predicted a tenfold increase. According to Viscount Leverhulme's calculations of 1919, the population of Lewis should by 1931 have been speeding along the road to 200,000 people, not dipping dangerously close to 20,000.

From the outset, the Stornoway Trust recognised and accepted its responsibilities in such a crisis. On 24 January 1924 Provost Kenneth Mackenzie told his fellow town councillors that the new Trust would invest 'in developments on or in connection with the Trust estate calculated to promote the material and social welfare of the community; in improving means of communication with the island by land, sea or air; in afforesting certain portions of the estate; in encouraging higher education by the provision of bursaries to enable deserving scholars to proceed to secondary schools and universities; in improving the medical service of the community by assisting in the employment of medical practitioners, equipping of hospitals or dispensaries; in the improvement or construction of roads and bridges'. It read more as the prospectus of a twentieth-century development agency than of a nineteenth-century Highland landowner, which was very much the point.

Lews Castle, Sir James Matheson's towering symbol of ownership, which some regarded as the jewel in the crown, should 'never be let as a hotel or club, nor as a private residence for a tenant of sporting rights'. It would become in due course a technical college, then a gigantic mouldering albatross, and finally a restored community asset and museum.

The Trust was established in the winter of 1923 and the early spring of 1924. That first edition of the Stornoway Trust would be composed of ten members. Five of them would be appointed *ex officio*, as established and elected members of the parent body of the enterprise, the Town Council. The other five would be directly elected to the Trust to represent 'those holding lands within the Trust area in their own right on tenure, or who appear in the Valuation Roll as paying rent for subjects within the said area in their own rights'.

The Representation of the People Act 1918 had given the vote in the United Kingdom to all men over the age of 21, regardless of their assets.

As a first gesture to the women's suffrage movement of the years before the First World War, it also enfranchised in parliamentary elections women over the age of 30, provided that they or their husbands occupied premises or land with an annual rateable value of more than £5. That extended franchise had applied to the newly formed parliamentary constituency of the Western Isles in the General Election of December 1918.

In such secondary democratic expressions as the elections for local government or in the 1921 Lewis prohibition referendum, equality of franchise was immediately granted. All women over the age of 21 were allowed to vote for town and county councillors, or for preventing Stornoway bars from serving drams, regardless of their family's rateable properties.

Those concessions were naturally taken to apply also to the first elections to the Stornoway Trust early in 1924, with the result that many women of Stornoway parish were entitled to vote for a Stornoway Trustee before they were permitted to elect a Member of Parliament.

Some women were also permitted by the 1918 Act to stand for office, but at first none of them did so. The candidates for the Stornoway Trust in 1924 were all men.

On Thursday 28 February 1924, polling stations across the north-eastern seaboard of the island of Lewis opened between eight 'in the forenoon' and eight 'in the afternoon'. There was a total of six such venues, at Aird and Bayble public schools in Point; at the infants' school of the Nicolson Institute and the Drill Hall on Church Street in Stornoway; at Back Public School and North Tolsta Public School in Broad Bay.

Inside them the adults of the communities were allowed to vote for a maximum of five from eleven candidates. They were Archibald MacArthur, a crofter from the small township of Steinish; Murdo Macaulay, another crofter from Sandwick; Angus MacKenzie, a flesher, or butcher, of Point Street in Stornoway; Donald G. Mackenzie, a draper of Cromwell Street; Norman Mackenzie, a merchant of Bayble in Point; Murdo MacLean, a commission agent of Lewis Street in Stornoway; George MacLeod, a crofter from Aignish in Point; John MacRitchie Morrison, a fish salesman of Francis Street in Stornoway; John Monro Pryde, a teacher of Francis Street; Angus Smith, the tenant farmer of Holm Farm; and John Pringle Tolmie, a doctor of Kenneth Street in Stornoway.

Voting was reported to be 'brisk'. It was variable. Certainly, some 295 people cast their ballots at the Nicolson Institute and the Drill Hall in Stornoway. Just thirty-two voters turned out in Point, and a mere thirteen at Back and Tolsta combined. Some, but very far from all, people from those far-flung suburbs and provinces will have voted in the town. One completed voting slip was rejected for having ticked more than the designated five candidates.

Despite the increased franchise, voter turnout in the Western Isles was low at all elections in the 1920s and 1930s. The General Elections of 1923 and 1924 persuaded, respectively, only 40 per cent and 39 per cent of the entire island electorate to cast a vote.

The turnout for the first Stornoway Trust election was even lower, attracting less than 10 per cent of the voting public. The reasons are not difficult to identify. Nobody had previously heard of the Stornoway Trust. There had not been a recognisable election campaign. The people of the town, and of Broad Bay and Point, had no real idea what they were voting for, or why. Voting for landowners was a concept so novel as to be bafflingly alien. Most adults in the depressed island of Lewis had other things to think and worry about.

Those who did bother to vote elected men of the professional classes, possibly because those voters themselves were of the professional classes, possibly because it was traditional in all quarters to choose professional men to represent island communities, and possibly because the professional men who were elected were well known, well liked and even admired.

The poll was topped by Dr John Pringle Tolmie with 193 votes. Tolmie was a general practitioner at the island's medical partnership on Kenneth Street in Stornoway. Doctor Jack, as he was known, had been born in Inverness forty-four years earlier, the son of David Tolmie, a Ross-shire grocer, and Margaret Pringle, a woman with Lewis connections from Rogart in Sutherland-shire. He was raised in both Inverness and Stornoway before joining the Kenneth Street practice when Dr Donald Murray became Medical Officer of Health for Lewis, and later the Liberal Member of Parliament for the Western Isles. Tolmie replaced Murray in partnership with Dr Murdoch Mackenzie. Drs Mackenzie and Murray had both died in their early 60s in 1922 and 1923 respectively, leaving Jack Tolmie, for a short time, as the only qualified physician in the town of Stornoway.

Just behind Tolmie, with 172 votes, was John MacRitchie Morrison. A 55-year-old native of Stornoway, Morrison was known in the town as an auctioneer of the fish landed in bulk at the pier. Throughout most of late-nineteenth- and early-twentieth-century Stornoway, that had been a rewarding pursuit which enabled John Morrison to raise his family in a comfortable house on Kenneth Street.

Murdo MacLean attracted 164 votes. A shipping agent,

and another son of Stornoway, the 53-year-old MacLean was credited in Lewis for having handled efficiently and with sensitivity the bookings and arrangements for the emigrants on the *Metagama* in the previous spring. He had also been provost of Stornoway when Leverhulme first arrived and became a staunch ally of the landowner.

Norman Mackenzie, who took 119 votes, was a 63-year-old ex-soldier from the large tidal island of Bernera off the west coast of Lewis. As a younger man Mackenzie had married the daughter of a Bayble storekeeper. When he finally departed the army – in which he had served for almost forty years, from 1880 until the last months of the Great War – they settled in Point and assumed ownership and management of the shop from Molly Mackenzie's parents.

The fifth and final candidate to duck under the rope with 102 votes was Angus Smith, the tenant of the small estate farm at Holm, east of Stornoway. A man from Uig in the west, the 53-year-old Smith had returned from a period in South Africa with a wife and two daughters before taking on the tenancy of Holm Farm in 1910. He would retain it until 1936 when he retired to the town of Stornoway.

Those five directly elected men were joined on the Stornoway Trust by another five *ex officio* volunteers from Stornoway Town Council.

The 54-year-old Hugh Macleod was not only a bailie and town councillor. He was also a trained accountant who had been factor, or chamberlain, of the entire Lewis estate for several years before and during the Leverhulme years – an inside position which led to Macleod becoming the first private owner of the newly carved up Galson estate. Yet another Stornoway man who was born and bred in the town and had raised his family in the estate's tied Mill Glen House,

MacLeod's knowledge of the inner workings of the property was probably unsurpassed.

John Louis Bain was another bailie and another product of Victorian Stornoway. He had been a clerk, a coal merchant, a fish curer and a shipping agent. Bain was also a native of the town who at the time of the Trust's formation was in his early 50s. A keen footballer and president of the Stornoway Bowling and Tennis Club, Louis Bain would become provost of Stornoway in 1925.

Roderick Smith was 50 years old in 1923 and had already served as the town's provost. A trained pharmacist, Roddy Smith left a substantial commercial and administrative legacy in Lewis. One of his town-centre businesses was still trading in the twenty-first century, and Smith himself served on the Town Council for fifty years from 1911 to the 1960s, having been twice made provost.

Councillor Samuel Ranger was a 60-year-old painter and decorator from Lochalsh on the western Highland mainland who had married a woman from South Lochs. The couple moved to Stornoway, where they made their home, raised their family, and established his business.

The first Trustees were chaired by the serving provost of Stornoway, Kenneth Mackenzie. That established the precedent for all future provosts of Stornoway to be automatically placed in the top chair at the Stornoway Trust, until 1981, when the office of provost was abandoned and James MacRae became the directly elected chair. Kenneth Mackenzie came from a South Lochs family. He had become a fish curer and coal merchant. In 1901 he had begun to establish in Lewis Street a cooperage to make barrels for the local fishing industry. He then changed his mind and installed carding and spinning machinery instead, and the emblematic name of twentieth-century Harris tweed was born. Another man who was twice made provost, Kenneth Mackenzie, was one of the founders of modern Lewis.

Every single one of those ten men was bilingual in Gaelic and English. They had to be. According to the National Census of 1921, in that year more than 70 per cent of the population of Stornoway spoke Gaelic. In the outlying crofting districts the percentage rose to 100: in Point and Broad Bay everybody spoke Gaelic and many people spoke only Gaelic.

When they met, however, the Trustees conducted their business in English. And so it was that in the middle of the 1920s the new body found itself discussing in English a matter which would have been anathema to Viscount Leverhulme – how to be one of the biggest, the best and most supportive of crofting landlords.

4

Crofts Fit for Heroes

The creation of new crofts in the Highlands and Islands of Scotland had been a relatively uncontroversial political ambition long before Viscount Leverhulme appeared in the Western Isles. Such initiatives had been underway ever since the passing of the Crofters Act of 1886. Under Conservative, Liberal and Labour governments, wrote James Hunter in *The Making of the Crofting Community*, 'the land settlement programme was an immediate and conspicuous success':

> Between 1886 and the early 1950s some 52,000 acres of arable land and 732,000 acres of pasture were added to the area occupied by crofters – a process which involved the creation of 2,742 new holdings and the enlargement of 5,160 previously existing crofts.
>
> The Crofters Commission and the Congested Districts Board (Scotland) had contributed to this total. But the greater part of it must be attributed to the endeavours of the Board of Agriculture in the years immediately following the First World War.
>
> And not only had more land been made available to crofters: sheep stocks had been taken over from

outgoing farmers and managed with considerable success; financial and agricultural aid to crofters everywhere had been increased; the improvement in agricultural techniques and in housing conditions – first apparent in the immediate aftermath of the Crofters Act of 1886 – had been maintained, indeed accelerated.

Most of the new crofts mentioned by Hunter, over 2,000 of them, were created in the immediate post-war years of 1919 to 1927, and the great bulk of them were staked out in the west Highlands and Islands. It was a signature of the times.

Three years before the war, in 1911, the minority Liberal government of Herbert Asquith passed a Small Landholders (Scotland) Act. Its function was 'to encourage the formation of small agricultural holdings in Scotland and to amend the law relating to the tenure of such holdings (including crofters' holdings)'. The 1911 Act was largely perceived as an attempt to extend the rights hard won by Highland and Island crofters to tenant farmers and smallholders throughout the rest of Scotland, which was its own mute compliment to the success of crofting.

It was also acknowledged that if the revered 1886 Crofting Act – and therefore the crofting system itself as currently legislated – had faults, they lay in its failure to provide for the tens of thousands of landless cottars in the Highlands and Islands. Following the 1886 Act, those who were lucky enough already to be crofters were granted their precious fair rents and security of tenure. But the large minority who were not crofters still had nothing. In the early 1920s there were as many as 2,000 such people squatting uncomfortably and unhappily in the estate of the Stornoway Trust alone.

Calum 'Safety' Smith, a future Stornoway Trustee, would write of his own family's experience of losing a croft on the west side of Lewis when he was a boy after the Great War, of their subsequent life in a barn, and then in a series of cramped and unhealthy hovels in the townships around Stornoway. Such landless cottars and squatters were often, then and later, misrepresented as destitutes and even beggars. They were more often than not ordinary, hardworking individuals, frequently younger sons without heritable tenancies and their families struggling to get by on the pay from daily piecework. Their need for the security of a croft would have been apparent at any time; in the hungry years between the wars it was urgent.

'It was of course the First World War that started it on a big scale,' wrote Calum Smith in the *Stornoway Gazette* in 1955.

> The returned warriors, especially the younger sons who were landless and tired of 'roaming with a hungry heart', wanted nothing more than to settle down on their native heath; and that is what many of them did. They staked their claims in common ground and were not to be gainsaid by stay-at-homes: and although their activities were watched by jealous and resentful eyes in some instances, they felt that they had fought for their privileges and – what impressed those who would oppose them – they looked as though they were prepared to do a lot more fighting. Furthermore they had many ex-servicemen friends among the crofters too, for when you have fought side by side along with a man, whether on land or sea, whatever the traditional attitude dictates, the human tendency is to see things with the same eyes.
>
> And so on the common pastures of almost all the townships of these islands the squatters established

themselves, many of them doing really excellent work with the unpromising materials on which they started. Taking over land which had produced nothing since the peat was skinned from it but heather, moss and poor-quality grass, they dug it up, trenched it, worked it into productive agricultural units which are today in some cases producing far more than neighbouring crofts.

'The old order changeth, yielding place to new' – and it changes because it is the pioneer in thoughts and deeds who alters the order of things. Among the squatters and plot-holders of these islands there are many of the pioneering type: men who made the barren soil fertile – and yet in law their children have not the right to inherit these plots of earth . . .

'The genius raids, but the common people occupy and possess.' And the common people who occupied and possessed the barren land and made it fertile, who built houses and grew good crops by their own labours, who made oases where there were deserts, will leave the abiding earth the richer for their passing through it.

The 1911 Act was ultimately unfit for the purpose of helping such people because between 1914 and 1918 focus shifted to global events, and because even in the crofting counties it was toothless. The 1911 Act could persuade, but not oblige, Scotland's major landowners to create smallholdings and, by and large, Scotland's major landowners were reluctant to do so. As the Ayrshire man Sheriff David Brand of the Crofters Commission had told the Scottish Secretary in 1903, most Highland landowners were set firmly against dispersing even a small part of their property into new crofts, 'no matter how serious the congestion on their estates, and no matter how poor and sterile the land presently is in occupation of the Crofting tenants'.

Public opinion changed some minds, and as the social historian Leah Leneman pointed out in *Fit for Heroes? Land Settlement in Scotland After World War I*, as the sacrifices in the Atlantic Ocean and on the Western Front sunk into the national consciousness following the end of the Great War, opposition to land settlement 'would have been considered unpatriotic'.

Nonetheless, Scottish landowners' intransigence, coupled with the concentrated monopoly of private Scottish landholding, severely restricted the country's early forays into land reform and redistribution. In Australia at that time, 40,000 settlers were given new holdings. In Denmark, 26,000 smallholdings were created. In England and Wales, county councils established 17,000 small agricultural properties. The 2,700 new crofts and 5,000 enlarged holdings in Scotland which were later hailed by James Hunter represented valuable steps in the right direction but were clearly insufficient in both local and international contexts. Throughout twentieth- and twenty-first-century Scotland, the practice of land reform constantly lagged a long way behind political rhetoric.

Towards the end of the Great War, with Lloyd George's 'homes fit for heroes' pledge ringing in their ears, politicians discussed an Act of Parliament which would give a newly formed Board of Agriculture in Scotland powers of compulsory purchase, with a view to buying, in part or in whole, large farms and agricultural estates and breaking them up into crofts or other smallholdings. That was a direction of travel in the opposite lane to the traffic of the previous two centuries, which saw smaller holdings subsumed into large farms and sheep ranches, and crofts emptied and abolished altogether.

It had radical implications for the Hebrides. In the words of James Hunter, 'In June 1917, the Board of Agriculture began preparing a Lewis land settlement scheme which was to be enacted at the end of the war and which was to involve practically every scrap of the island's potentially arable land. Lewis then being up for sale, the government actually considered buying it in its entirety.' At that point William Hesketh Lever stepped into the picture and removed Lewis from the open market.

It was not immediately clear how fiercely the new landowner disliked crofting. As it became obvious that Leverhulme not only opposed the creation of new crofts but wished also to abolish those in existence, Scottish politicians settled down for the long haul. They would temporarily pause new settlement schemes in Lewis. They would not, however, prosecute land raiders or withdraw the long-term objective of giving Lewis people a toehold on their land. If Leverhulme's grand industrialisations failed to work or were withdrawn, all bets would be off.

Dr Donald Murray devoted his maiden speech in the House of Commons to the subject. On the evening of Monday, 18 March 1919, three months after his election, the new Western Isles MP rose to his feet and told his parliamentary colleagues that 'The people connected with the Highlands were promised a more active administration of the [land settlement] Acts as soon as the war was over.

'... the men of the Highlands and Islands are coming back in their hundreds. Land has been promised them on many estates, especially in the Western Isles, and they want to know whether these promises are going to be fulfilled. The

Government promised, the Secretary for Scotland promised, and the officials of the Board of Agriculture promised that, when the war was over, these matters should be settled.

'I quite admit the difficulties of the situation while the war was going on. But many of these men have been home for a long time. The Armistice was signed many months ago, and as far as the people can see, the Board of Agriculture are doing nothing towards the redemption of their promises to divide up some of these lands among the people who have sent in applications for them.

'In the old days when young men in the Highlands were sent away to the war, they were promised land on their return, but when they did come back they not only got no land, but in many instances they found the homes of their fathers were burnt to the ground and their families deported to America and Australia. Of course, that sort of thing can never occur again.

'But still there is a suspicion running through the mind of the people and they want to see action taken. One ground for this suspicion – I do not say I believe it myself – is that there is such a large number of [Conservative] Unionist Members in this House, and there is an idea abroad in the Highlands that the Unionist party have always been associated with opposition to proper schemes of land reform to the Highlands.

'Of course, that is not universally believed, and I know that many Unionist Members of this House are as anxious to see a settlement of the land question as any Radical. It is up to them to remove that suspicion and not to clog the efforts of the Secretary for Scotland or the Board of Agriculture, but rather to stimulate them in the administration of those clauses of the Land Acts which provide for the creation of small holdings in the Highlands and Islands of Scotland.

'Sometimes it is said there is no demand in the country for small holdings. I cannot speak for the whole of Scotland, but I can speak for my own constituency, and I can say that in the Western Isles, without going into details, there are about 2,000 applications already in for small holdings there. If I may be permitted to invade the constituency of my right honourable friend the Solicitor-General for Scotland [Thomas Brash Morison, the Inverness MP], I can add 400 applications sent in from the island of Skye.

'We are hearing a great deal about reconstruction. Of course, reconstruction has a very large and wide meaning in big industrial areas in the south. But the first stone in the foundation of reconstruction in the Highlands and Islands is a proper settlement of the land question . . .'

The island's former chief medical officer continued: 'In the island of Lewis, the dominant partner in the Western Isles, which has a population of about 30,000, about 800 applications have been sent in for land during the last eight or nine years. I think I am right in saying that not one of those applications has yet been granted. I am sorry to say that many of the men who sent in applications some years ago will not return to enjoy the land for which they fought.

'The Board of Agriculture have promised us a farm called Gress, to which I drew the attention of the right honourable Gentleman [the Scottish Secretary of State] some time ago.

'Applications were sent in from neighbouring townships for that farm. That was some eight years ago. The usual inquiries were made. I hope the right honourable Gentleman will not tell me that inquiries will be made in regard to these holdings. It is not necessary, because all these cases have been inquired into over and over again. The pigeon-holes of the Board of Agriculture are stuffed with reports of their officials on these cases, and there is no need to go beyond the office to settle these questions. To quote a remark from a speech made by the right honourable Gentleman himself, which appeared in the papers to-day and which he delivered in practical Scotland, "The time for talk is passed; now is the time for deeds."

'I would like to give a serious warning to the Secretary for Scotland. I hope the House will believe that I am a man of peace and that the men of the Western Isles do not want any disturbance if they can avoid it. I should deprecate anything of that sort, and so far as my influence can and could go it has been going and will go on the side of peace.

'But I warn the Secretary for Scotland on the matter. I would rather like the Board of Agriculture to anticipate any direct action. Some thousands of these men have been at the war and learned the value of direct action, just as much as the men in your big industrial centres.

'I am perfectly certain that the principle of direct action will be followed in these cases, just as freely and with more effect than in your industrial centres.'

Donald Murray was a Leòdhasach and a member of the Liberal Party. The man who followed him in that debate in 1919 was a King's Counsel from Renfrewshire and the Conservative and Unionist Member of Parliament for Glasgow Springburn. In his anxiety to allay suspicions about Tories and to establish street credibility for his party, nothing better illustrated the widespread post-war support for land reform and renewed land settlement than the contribution of Frederick Alexander Macquisten, KC, MP.

'Our Glasgow constituencies,' said the Springburn Conservative MP, 'are full of men whose fathers and grand-fathers were driven out by the crucifixion of the people of the Highlands and Islands upon the rights of property, and extreme exercise of the land laws which drove them forth, and indignation still burns in our great industrial centres when they recollect how many thousands of men were driven out of the Highlands and Islands of Scotland for the purpose of making sheep runs which in later years when sheep failed became deer forests.

'That is why any step which the Secretary for Scotland may take, no matter how drastic, which will enable every one of these sturdy fishermen to find a croft with which to supplement his fishing will be supported.

'Many of them go to sea in ships, and come home to their holdings, which they till, just as you find done on the coast of Norway. Every one of these men is a naval reserve man, and every one of them answered to the nation's call . . .

'What we want, as the Member for the Western Islands has warned us, is to remember that the men coming back from the front may not be so submissive as the men who came back from Waterloo were when they found that their fathers' farm houses had been burned . . .'

The Scottish Secretary noted the strong feelings of both men. He asked for time to win the consent of the new landowner and pointed out that 'the Board has recently purchased land in Skye and elsewhere, some of which it is hoped may be available to mitigate congestion in the Island of Lewis'.

Robert Munro was referring to a new settlement at Portnalong, in a district of north-western Skye which had been cleared 100 years earlier. In 1919 and 1920 the UK government, through the Board of Agriculture, negotiated and paid Norman MacLeod of Dunvegan, whose family had originally cleared the place, £58,609 for 60,000 acres of sheep ranch in the Talisker region of Bracadale. That deal led to the anomaly of the first official crofting resettlement of Lewis people after the Great War being across the Minch in Skye. They came from Point, a part of Lewis which would soon afterwards become the responsibility of the Stornoway Trust. Portnalong was staked out into sixty-eight crofts. Forty-three of them were assigned to land-hungry Harrismen, five to Skye crofters and twenty to applicants from the Point peninsula in Lewis. At its inception the new township had approximately 400 residents.

It was unusual to resettle landless Hebrideans in different islands. It would have been culturally insensitive in any era, but in the early years of the twentieth century it evoked unpleasant recollections of Highlanders being deported to different continents. Harris people were, however, notoriously difficult to rehouse within their small, stony island. Lewis men and women should not, on the face of things, have experienced such problems in the largest offshore island of the British Isles. Wherever they looked in Lewis they saw wide open, empty spaces.

Those twenty Rubhaich crofters and their families who were transplanted to new holdings in Portnalong therefore represented a failure of central government of which Robert Munro and Donald Murray were well aware. The few dozen people from Point nonetheless made the best of their circumstances and tried to resume their old familiar lifestyles in Skye. A couple of years after the settlement, a Board of Agriculture official from Portnalong reported, '12 of the Lewismen and 7 Lewis girls went as hired hands to the English herring fishing this year and have just returned home . . .'

Liz Sutherland, the daughter of Lewis parents who grew up in Portnalong, told Leah Leneman in 1988, 'When they went to the fishing they went in May or June and they were home at the end of August, that was the summer season. And then, in October, they would go away to the winter fishing down south, down in Yarmouth and that ... And they were away until November. And then he was home in the wintertime but he had a small boat himself and him and my brother did white fishing and lobster fishing and they sent the lobsters to Billingsgate.

'The ones that went to the herring fishing it was all Lewis people, but nearly every one of the Harris people and some of the Lewis people went to the salmon fishing in Perth in the summertime.'

Portnalong refuted the old suspicion that, like hothouse flowers, Hebrideans could not successfully be transplanted in other islands. On the contrary: Liz Sutherland's father regarded his family's new croft in Skye as 'a dream come true'. Liz had often heard her mother say that when they were in Lewis they were crowded together so closely that 'when the hens got out they went in my grandfather's corn'. There had not been anywhere to graze the cow so her grandmother had to take her to the shieling some 30 miles away. Coming to Skye where they had so much space was a liberation for them. She also remembered what a happy community spirit there was until she left in the 1960s – a community spirit which was certainly assisted by the fact that all the Hearaich came from the same small island, and all of the Leòdhasaich came from Point.

It was nonetheless preferable for people to be settled in their home island, especially when that island was chronically underpopulated.

Within the old parish bounds, the Stornoway Trust inherited the stewardship of 1,307 crofts in Broad Bay, Point, and the satellite townships which circled the town. Those numbers were almost immediately increased in 1922 when Viscount Leverhulme had pulled the plug from Lewis industrial development. The Scottish Office and the Board of Agriculture took that as their cue and promptly created new crofts all across Leverhulme's properties.

On the east coast, within Stornoway parish, the farm which for seventy years since 1852 had stood on cleared ground north of Tolsta was dissolved into crofts, and renamed as the settlement of Baile Ùr Tholastaidh, or New Tolsta.

Five miles down the Broad Bay coast at Gress, the local farm was also broken up and forty-six crofts were created. Gress Farm had been a bone of contention for years. The historian Bill Lawson notes in *Lewis in History and Legend: The East Coast* that 'Gress was unusual in the land raids in that the farm had never been crofted and cleared, but had always been a farm'. It was nonetheless a prized piece of land before and after the war, as Donald Murray MP had suggested in his maiden speech in parliament.

Four miles south of Gress, at the same time the farm at Upper Coll was converted into forty-two crofts. At Eagleton in Lower Bayble in Point twenty new crofts were staked out.

Between 1919 and 1927, 251 new crofts were created in the whole of the island of Lewis, most of them on the estate of the Stornoway Trust, and 276 holdings were enlarged.

A couple of hundred new crofts would not satisfy all of the 800 applicants in Lewis, who had been mentioned by Donald Murray MP in 1919, even though 250 crofters could represent 1,000 people or more, given that crofters were usually family men. Moreover, that achievement was overshadowed by the neighbouring island group of Skye and Raasay, where in the same eight years 313 crofts were established and 147 were enlarged.

But it was a start, and if it was a gesture it was a significantly friendly gesture. Those developments and others represented hope and stability to hundreds of people on the land which was to be administered by the Stornoway Trust. Such reforms were not limited to one part of the Highlands and Islands, or even to one parish of Lewis. They occurred throughout the north and west of Scotland, and they dictated the tone, the economy and the culture of that vast region for the next century.

In Lewis as much as, if not more than, anywhere else in the north-west of the British Isles, it was to be a crofting century. '[D]espite all the attention given to the Leverhulme period,' wrote Professor Ewen Cameron of the University of Edinburgh in 1996, 'the most noticeable point about it has been ignored by past historians. This is the fact that, despite the strong opposition of the proprietor, practically all the available farmland in Lewis was, in fact, eventually utilised for land settlement.'

A secure, independent, broadly egalitarian, communal, free and healthy way of life was established from Shetland to the Mull of Kintyre.

For the greater part of that century, only on 68,000 acres of eastern Lewis was that lifestyle nurtured by a suitable and sympathetic landlord.

It was not a smooth journey. In 1924 some established crofters on Stornoway Trust land in Point objected to the Trust's proposal to resume sixteen acres of land to provide permanent homes for a handful of squatting cottars on the Knock and Swordale common grazings. Five of the cottars 'had taken possession of the land and . . . had erected thereon more or less substantial houses'.

The matter found its way to the Scottish Land Court, which in September 1924 found in favour of the Trust.

'While we do not give any countenance to the practice of squatting, which we believe to be a violation of the law and one which has been responsible for a great deal of the congestion which is so deplorable a feature of life in Lewis, we cannot shut our eyes to the benefits likely to accrue from schemes which attempted to put it upon a proper basis.

'One of the objects of the [Stornoway Trust] scheme is to legalise and put under proper conditions and restraints the use of the land.

'If that is so,' ruled the Land Court, mischievously asking the protesting crofters to remember their own recent history, 'it does not well beseem the crofters themselves to object to this process, for they are responsible for the existence of this state of matters, and have encouraged, if they have not created, the practice of squatting in opposition to and against the wishes of the estate officials, who have always set their faces against it.

'But as these men have been occupying part of this pasture at least with the concurrence of the rest of the crofters in the township, it is not in their mouth to represent that the mere regularising of their position, and the limitation of their activities to a prescribed and curtailed portion of the land, could form such a serious injury to their rights.'

Nor did the land raids cease overnight. In the spring of 1929, on the tenth anniversary of the first raids on Lord Leverhulme's properties in Broad Bay, some twenty men raided Melbost Farm and staked out claims for new crofts.

Melbost stands to the east of Stornoway, between the town and the crofting peninsula of Point, with which district it is closely associated. The men embarked on their spring raid after demanding for several years that the Board of Agriculture and the Stornoway Trust should dismantle Melbost Farm as they had broken up its equivalents at Tolsta and Gress. The tenancy lease of Melbost expired in 1929 and the Board had indicated that it was prepared at that point 'to take the farm under their compulsory powers for the purpose of enlarging existing small holdings and forming new ones'.

The landowner demurred, and on this occasion the landowner was a democratically elected local body. The Board duly backed away from Melbost, and the aspiring crofters from the district planned their raids.

It was a small but significant moment. The surface issue was the same as in Leverhulme's time: the Stornoway milk supply. In the 1920s the town imported 200 gallons of milk daily from mainland Scotland. The Trust intended to renew its lease at Melbost with a farmer who would devote the land to dairy cattle. The reliable provision of farmed dairy products did not much concern the crofting hinterlands, where household milking cows were commonplace. It was however increasingly important to the town of Stornoway, for whose people the Trust was also responsible and to whose voting feuholders and ratepayers the Trustees were also answerable.

Shortly before the raids the matter of Melbost was raised in the House of Commons by the Labour MP for Dundee, Tom Johnston. Johnston asked the Secretary of State for Scotland whether, 'seeing that he issued recently a statutory notice to the proprietors of Melbost farm, Stornoway, of his intention to proceed with a compulsory scheme of land settlement on the farm, and that within 72 hours afterwards a further notice was served cancelling the first and indicating his intention not to proceed with the settlement, he will say what steps he now proposes to take to provide holdings for landless men in that area?'

The Scottish Secretary, the Glasgow Pollok MP Sir John Gilmour, replied that the statutory notice had been a delaying device, 'which was issued in order to postpone the conclusion of arrangements for a new lease pending further discussion with the owners as to the future use of the lands . . . it is not intended to continue proceedings for the development of a small holding scheme if it can be shown that under a new lease the lands will be used for dairying.

'With regard to the last part of the question,' concluded Sir John, 'I would remind the honourable Member that, with the exception of this relatively small subject and the Manor Farm owned by the Stornoway Trustees and used for dairying, all available agricultural subjects in Lewis have been secured for small holdings schemes.'

Melbost Farm survived. A tightrope had been walked between the needs of the town and the demands of the country. The Stornoway Trust had asserted itself as an independent adjudicator which was prepared to take difficult decisions on behalf of all its constituents.

That would not be the last time it trod on broken glass at Melbost.

5

The First in the Field

Not least because he still owned the largest part of the island, and was making familiar noises about grandiose developments down south in Harris, the presence of Viscount Leverhulme continued to haunt Lewis until the spring of 1925.

The union flag which flew over Lews Castle was lowered to half-mast on 7 May of that year, giving many in Stornoway their 'first intimation of the sad intelligence', although news spread through the town like a muirburn.

In the last week of April Leverhulme had gone down with a chill which developed into pneumonia. He died at his home in the London borough of Hampstead in the early hours of the morning of Thursday, 7 May 1925. He was 73 years old.

On 11 May William Hesketh Lever, Viscount Leverhulme of the Western Isles, was buried beside his wife at Port Sunlight, the model workers' village he had built in the late 1880s on the opposite bank of the Mersey estuary to the city of Liverpool, in the days before he got into the swing of having places named after himself.

On the Monday of his funeral all shops were closed in Lewis. Shortly after midday the Nicolson Institute sent its students home, and the Lewis Pipe Band paraded on the terrace before the castle playing the laments 'Lochaber No More', 'The Flowers of the Forest' and 'Cumha nam Marbh'.

Stornoway's United Free English Church held a joint religious service. Reverend Donald John Macinnes told the congregation: 'Our chief interest in Lord Leverhulme is the connection he had of late years with ourselves as proprietor of the Long Island. His schemes and ideals for Lewis miscarried, and there may be differences of opinion as to the causes of failure. A man of his career and experience would be more than human if he did not sometimes want his own way and a free hand; but no one can imagine that he had selfish ends in view.

'He was genuinely anxious to do the best he could for the people. There is no reason to doubt the sincerity of his words when he said that he loved the Lewis people.'

Other than the single millennial establishment of the Stornoway Trust, Leverhulme had made no provision whatsoever for the future of his substantial holdings in Harris and Lewis in the event of his death. Beyond the parish of Stornoway there was to be no bequested body devoted to the care of the islands and the continuance of what developments had survived.

On the contrary, he had signed an agreement with Lever Brothers which absolved them of any responsibilities in the Hebrides. As just another part of his personal estate they would be inherited by his son, the second Viscount Leverhulme, who, as his father knew, had no affection for the islands.

Lever Brothers and the new Viscount Leverhulme instantly pulled the plug on Lewis and Harris. All developments in Harris were halted and all employees were given a week's notice. The new chairman and board pounced with indecent haste upon the opportunity to consolidate their real assets. As the old man himself had foreseen, the time for the company to relax and cease from adventurous enterprise arrived with his death.

Rural Lewis beyond the embrace of the Stornoway Trust was parcelled up and sold off piecemeal as a series of small individual estates. Shortly afterwards, Colin MacDonald of the Board of Agriculture and the Glasgow physician Halliday Sutherland arrived separately in Harris. Writing of the settlement of Obbe, which its township fathers had renamed to honour their new proprietor, MacDonald observed, 'Leverburgh never attained the status of a town. Just a score or so of houses and some scars on the moor (now healed by kindly time and vegetation) where streets and buildings were meant to be.

'And the pier – that imposing structure of piles and planks that seemed to cover acres. Three years ago, when I landed there off a motor boat from Berneray the piles were rotting and the planks sagging to such an extent that we were glad to get off them onto firm land.'

'At Obbe,' reported Sutherland of the same place in the 1930s, 'there is now no industry, some of the houses built by Leverhulme have been bought by retired officials, others are occupied by squatters, and one of the half-built villas is used as a cow byre by a crofter living in a black house.'

'Those who believe,' Dr Leah Leneman concluded in 1989, 'that Lewis would have been transformed if Leverhulme had been left alone to get on with his plans, have not looked at Harris.'

The men who sat around a table in Stornoway as trustees of a substantial community landowner in the early months of 1924 had no model, no guidebook, no precedents, no rehearsal. Unlike such community ventures later in the twentieth and into the twenty-first centuries, who were by then able to look at the Stornoway Trust for a wide variety of exemplars, the first elected guardians of the Stornoway Trust itself were obliged to write their own script.

There were several nationalised estates in the Highlands and Islands of Scotland, which were bought and operated by the British state through such devolved Scottish bodies as the Congested Districts Board and the Board of Agriculture. They included the estate in Skye which contained a few score Rubhaich on new crofts in the township of Portnalong. They were largely uncontroversial and responsible enterprises which earned their tenantry's respect and survived comfortably into the twenty-first century.

Before 1924 there was, however, only one established community landowner. The category difference was important. State and community ownership were each a different way of removing parts of northern Scotland, one estate at a time, from the dead hands of private ownership. But whereas the vast wealth, personnel and expertise of the British state could hardly fail to operate and underwrite a few Highland and Hebridean properties, community ownership of the same properties was far more fragile. As the members of the Lewis District Committee discovered in 1923, without substantial reserves community landowners were wide open to personal and organisational bankruptcy, in which case their precious hills, machair land and townships would be straight back on the open market at a knockdown price, the failed experiment having bequeathed only poverty and the bitterness of broken dreams.

In the remote north-west of the island of Skye, the Glendale estate had been bought for £15,000 by the Congested Districts (Scotland) Commission from its private owner in 1904, and their holdings, including the common grazings, were sold to Glendale crofters in 1908. There had been considerable unrest in Glendale in the 1880s and relationships between the common people and the local landowning class did not quickly heal.

Otherwise the estates of Glendale and Stornoway had little in common. Glendale, at 23,000 acres, was around a third of the size of the Stornoway Trust's territory. But the Skye property had just 147 crofters and fewer than 1,000 people in total, as set against the 10,000 urban and rural residents of Broad Bay, Point and Greater Stornoway. There was no town hall, no chartered royal burgh and no business community beyond the shop and post office in Glendale, only a handful of small townships. There was no sheltered deep-water port and harbour, just an exposed fishing jetty in Loch Pooltiel. The crofters of Glendale became owner-occupying smallholders who kept their grazings in common and were shareholders in the estate. The crofters of eastern Lewis remained tenants of a locally elected trust. Even if ten professional Lewismen had stooped to look for lessons across the Minch in Skye, they would have found vanishingly few.

As an accountable community landowner, with no predecessors, no older siblings and no state support, the Stornoway Trust was alone in a predatory world.

It did not take the hard-headed Lewis businessmen on the Trust long to realise that the bricks-and-mortar assets, urban amenities and commercial enterprises inherited from Viscount Leverhulme were very far from money spinners.

They primarily amounted to the Stornoway Fish Processing Company, the Fish Offal Works and the Lewis Steam Laundry, all of which had been established by Leverhulme, the Stornoway Gas Company and the policies, gardens, grounds and massive edifice of Lews Castle, which had fallen into his hands as parts of the Lewis estate.

Since the decline of the fisheries industry, the first four made little if any money, while the last one, the castle, simply ate up cash. Leverhulme knew that: it was why, in his own words, he had transferred ownership of the fish and gas and laundry works to the Stornoway Trust, 'the income from which to go towards the maintenance and upkeep of the Castle and Policies and Gardens, and for these purposes only, solely and entirely for none other'.

The problem was, after the requirements of the castle had been satisfied there was then no money left for the Trust to invest in 'improving means of communication with the island by land, sea or air; in afforesting certain portions of the estate; in encouraging higher education by the provision of bursaries to enable deserving scholars to proceed to secondary schools and universities; in improving the medical service of the community by assisting in the employment of medical practitioners, equipping of hospitals or dispensaries; in the improvement or construction of roads and bridges', as the ambitious prospectus of the Stornoway Trust had detailed for itself.

There was in fact no disposable profit at all, and there would be none until well into the 1930s. The Stornoway Trust was in the unexpected condition of being dependent not on free enterprise, but on the independently adjudicated and fixed annual subsistence rental from its 1,500 crofters, which at an average of less than £2 per croft amounted in most years to less than £6,000. It did not help that in those hungry years, as the Trust would admit, 'considerable difficulty was experienced in collecting the rent'.

And then there was the castle. While preparing his bequest to a Stornoway Trust, Viscount Leverhulme had envisioned a suitably grand future for his former Hebridean mansion home as a political and cultural hub of the island and the official residence of a head of the Lewis state. He had therefore ring-fenced its potential use with provisions and qualifications. Those provisions were summarised by the *Northern Ensign* in the first month of 1924.

> There is a condition in the Castle trust that the Castle shall never be let as a hotel or club, nor as a private residence for a tenant of sporting rights, but provision is made that a portion of the Castle shall be used to house a library, museum, and art gallery, to be opened free to the public.
>
> A portion of it shall also be used for a town hall and municipal offices, and the trustees shall, from time to time offer sufficient accommodation in the Castle to the Provost of the Burgh of Stornoway for the time being for use as an official residence, and, in the event of the Provost accepting such accommodation, he shall receive an allowance from the trust of £500 per annum on account of additional expenses to which he may be put in respect of such occupancy.
>
> The substantial castle grounds should, in Leverhulme's prescription, become a public park.

Without the permission of the UK Parliament or of the Court of Session, the Trustees were forbidden from selling any part of the property.

A sub-committee known as the Castle Trust would be established to manage the castle's affairs and to remit all profits to their overlords at the Stornoway Trust. 'The trustees of the Castle trust will consist of: The Provost and Magistrates of the Burgh of Stornoway.'

But of course, there were no profits from Lews Castle and its grounds, which comprised 700 acres of woodland, grassland, lawn and exotic imported plants. There was only substantial and chronic expenditure. Stornoway certainly needed a new town hall. The existing building had been gutted by fire in 1918, but the castle was equally certainly unsuitable for such a function. Ultimately the established town hall was rebuilt and restored to use in 1929. The provosts of the burgh already lived in comfortable town houses. They had no need of rooms in a castle a few hundred yards away, and no desire to be seen or to see themselves as presidents in palaces. Finally, there were in the 1920s neither the funds nor the demand for a museum and art gallery in Lews Castle. That and the use of the grounds as a public park were the only two of Leverhulme's ambitions for the property to be even partly realised, but the former took a further century.

Within a couple of years the Trustees realised that Lews Castle, which in district valuation was easily the most valuable single property in the Outer Hebrides, was dragging down the Stornoway Trust.

In the words of Helen Haugh, professor in Community Enterprise at the Cambridge Judge Business School, reporting, in 2021, on the Trust's early finances, 'The first accounts for the Trust list the capital gifted by Leverhulme (£33,485). The assets comprise heritable property (£26,905), Manor Farm (£3,281), shares in LDFA (£821) and land and rent arrears (£2,179).

'In the revenue account, income was received from land, house rents and feu duties (£4,946), and investments (£11). Principal costs incurred are the upkeep of Lews Castle and policies (£2,667), and shootings (£994). The Trust records a deficit of £5,612 in its first year.'

By the end of 1927, after its third full year of operation, it was estimated that the Trust could not depend on annual revenue of more than £5,800. 'It was also estimated,' the Edinburgh Court of Session heard in 1928, 'on the other hand, that if they retained the castle and policies, even with all possible reductions, their annual expenditure could not be less than £8,000.'

At that hearing in January 1928, the Court of Session was considering a petition in the name of Louis Bain, fish curer, and other members of the Stornoway Trust concerning their ownership of Lews Castle and its grounds. Louis Bain was in 1928 both the provost of Stornoway and chair of the Stornoway Trust of which he had been a founding member.

'The Stornoway trustees have carried on the trust for over three years,' the court was told, 'but since the beginning the working of the trust has resulted in considerable loss each year, and the petitioners stated that they were satisfied that under the present trust fetters there was no prospect of any free revenue being available in the future for any of the trust's purposes . . .

'The chief cause of the large annual debit appeared clearly to be the excessive cost of the maintenance and upkeep of the castle and policies, which the revenue derived . . . was quite inadequate to meet.'

The solution to this potentially fatal state of affairs, proposed Provost Louis Bain and his fellow Trustees, was for the Court of Session to adjust the terms of Viscount Leverhulme's bequest. 'To meet the difficulty,' reported *The Scotsman* newspaper, 'the petitioners asked for approval of a scheme which, inter alia, authorised them to sell or lease the castle and policies, this being in their view the only possible method of rendering the trust solvent.'

Before nodding the adjustment through, from the bench Lord Andrew Anderson asked the Stornoway Trust's legal counsel 'if this gift of Lord Leverhulme's is ever likely to be anything but a white elephant?'

He was told in reply that 'it does not appear to be otherwise, but if the trustees could dispose of the castle even for very little, they would be better off than with a wasting asset'.

Lews Castle, that formidable 'wasting asset', was not immediately sold or put out on a long-term lease – largely because in the late 1920s and 1930s it was far from easy to find a suitable buyer or lessee.

In June 1935 Messrs Cameron and Forrest of Inverness presented a ten-year audit of the Stornoway Trust 'covering the financial affairs of the Trust since its inception in 1924'.

The auditors reported: 'since the Trust was formed in 1924 there has always been a revenue surplus prior to disbursements being made in connection with the Lewis Castle and policies. In the early years the surplus was a small one, but with the reduction of the rating burden a considerable revenue surplus was achieved.'

Nonetheless, said Cameron and Forrest, the balance of each annual set of accounts was entirely determined 'by the amount spent on the upkeep of the castle and policies . . . In the early years of the Trust's working the accounts show that the revenue surplus was insufficient to meet the expenditure on the castle and policies, but from 1929 to 1933 inclusive there was a small surplus.'

They had been bequeathed a property which flattered to deceive, said the auditors.

'When the trustees took over there was a considerable deficit, which has never been wiped off.

'The main assets of the Trust are the crofters' rents and the feu-duties of Stornoway which represent a very considerable sum at their capitalised value. The main drain on the finances has been the upkeep of Lewis Castle and its spacious grounds, which serve the community as a public park.

'Some years ago, to lessen their burden, the trustees obtained authority from the Court of Session to sell or let the castle. The castle and fishings have generally been let since then but so far the trustees have been unable to effect a sale.'

They had survived. The dignity and good name of Stornoway was intact. The Trustees determined to tighten their collective belt, which was a familiar precaution to any child of the nineteenth-century Hebrides. They would continue to economise, especially in expenditure on Lews Castle and its grounds.

In 1928 the Stornoway Trust appointed a ground officer, a clerk, a full-time manager of its day-to-day affairs who became what the tenant crofters, then and forever after, would know as their estate factor. His name was Edwin Aldred. He was in his 30s, having been born in the mill town of Leigh in Lancashire in 1891. Aldred had arrived in Stornoway just a few years earlier as the manager of Leverhulme's Stornoway Fish Products and Ice Company, and the Lewis Island Preserved Specialities Company. Acting as the landowner's 'personal financial adviser', in the words of Ken Galloway of Stornoway Historical Society, 'Ed Aldred was directly involved in the financial administration' of Leverhulme's Lewis enterprise.

He was not a Gaelic speaker. He had no previous experience of the Hebrides, let alone of crofters and crofting. With such inauspicious qualifications, Edwin Aldred would nonetheless hold down his new job for almost forty years. In 1923 he married Catherine MacLennan of the MacLennan/'Coachie' family of Scotland Street. They had no children. Edwin Aldred retired from the Stornoway Trust only in 1960 when he was 68 years old.

In the middle of the 1920s, Edwin Aldred and his Trustees readied themselves for the long haul.

6

Aviators, Golfers and Crofters

On a fine morning in the summer of 1934, Captain Ernest Edmund 'Ted' Fresson flew a de Havilland *Dragon* biplane from Inverness over the Minch to Stornoway. On that auspicious occasion the eight-passenger capacity *Dragon* contained his engineer and four guests.

Ted Fresson was a Surrey man who had served in the precursor of the RAF, the Royal Flying Corps, during the First World War. After working in the young aviation industry of newly republican China, in the 1920s he returned to the United Kingdom and offered joy rides to paying customers between the makeshift airstrips which were being marked out across the British Isles. That inevitably took him to the north of Scotland, and in 1933 he established the Highland Airways aviation company.

By 1934 Ted Fresson was busily engaged in establishing regular civilian air services to the islands and remoter parishes of northern and western Scotland. Having earlier in the year launched scheduled flights to Wick in Caithness and Kirkwall in Orkney, 'My next attention,' he later recalled in *Air Road to the Isles*, 'was to survey the Stornoway route.'

I was anxious to get the whole of the north of Scotland tied up before outsiders started to poke their noses in. Already I had heard rumours of a southern aviation company having designing eyes on Stornoway, and I wanted to be in first.

A long conversation on the phone with my friend Kenny Ross at the Caledonian Hotel, Stornoway, ensued. He would mark off a 300 yard strip for me on the Melbost golf links in the direction of the prevailing wind. He said there would be two bunkers in the middle with only a thirty foot gap between – would that be alright?

'A bit close,' I said. 'The Dragon's wheels are around thirteen feet apart. That doesn't leave much room does it, Kenny?'

'Well, Captain, I don't see what we can do as there isn't another strip that long with a suitable surface.'

'Alright, Kenny,' I said. 'We'll have to make it do. Can you mark the top inside edge of the bunkers with a linen sheet and place one in between – in the middle of the run?'

'Certainly, Captain. We have plenty of old sheets in the hotel. I'll get that done.'

'Also,' I said, 'light a smoke fire as soon as I circle the golf links.'

'Yes, we'll do just that.'

Fresson was right about 'a southern aviation company having designing eyes on Stornoway'. In the spring of 1933 Midland & Scottish Air Ferries Ltd had approached the Stornoway Trust to inquire about 'suitable landing grounds' in the vicinity of the town. Air travel to and from anywhere, let alone to and from the island of Lewis, cannot have been envisioned when the Trustees were children, but it clearly fell into the Trust's founding commitment to 'improving means of communication', and they agreed wholeheartedly to cooperate.

Midland & Scottish operated from the old military facility of Renfrew Airport, by Glasgow. Founded in March 1933 by a couple who had run a Lanarkshire bus company, it operated fledgling services to the islands of Bute and Islay and had landed an exploratory aeroplane on the Traigh Mhor in Barra.

Like most of their successors in Highland airspace, Midland & Scottish Air Ferries were uncommonly good at self-promotion. In February 1934 the Aberdeen *Press and Journal* reported:

> Stornoway will probably have a three-day-a-week air service to Renfrew from next March onwards. The project has been under discussion for some time and everything has now been satisfactorily arranged.
>
> The landing ground will be on the tidal flats at the golf course, and the club has expressed its willingness for the area to be so used for a period of three years.
>
> The Steinish crofters have grazing rights on the ground, and the scheme will meantime operate with them in conjunction with Mr Aldred, factor to the Stornoway trustees, who will look after the interests of the superiors.
>
> It was subsequent to this arrangement being made that the Midland & Scottish Air Ferries intimated that they would commence an experimental service in March.
>
> The project is welcomed locally, not only because it will provide additional travel facilities to and from the

island, but because of the fact that Stornoway airport is likely to assist the tourist industry, to cater for which there has been recent large extrusion of hotel accommodation in the town.

It also believed that, with regular air connection with Glasgow, Stornoway will stand a good chance of being selected as the jumping-off stage for an Atlantic air service if that should ever come on the northern route.

In June 1934 the Trust applied to the Scottish Land Court to resume from common grazings thirty-two acres of land by Steinish 'for use as a landing field for aeroplanes concurrent with its present use for grazing purposes'.

Factor Edwin Aldred told the court that 'the application had been made following upon communications with the Midland & Scottish Air Ferries Ltd. Pilots from Air Ferries had on several occasions visited the district and selected the area in question as the only suitable landing field in the neighbourhood of Stornoway.

'Recently they had written to state that unless landing facilities were made available in Stornoway it would not be worth their while establishing a service to the Outer Islands at all.'

The application to resume pastureland from the crofters, Edwin Aldred emphasised, was not made on behalf of Air Ferries, 'but on behalf of the Stornoway Trustees, who would keep the ground for the use of all aeroplanes and charge landing dues. Any profits would go to the Trust funds, the surplus of which under the trust deed must be devoted to various charitable purposes.' What was more, the crofters would be fully financially compensated as if they were losing the thirty-two acres for good and forever, instead of being asked to share the turf with a couple of aeroplanes each week.

The Steinish crofters, who did not see themselves as the main beneficiaries of Stornoway becoming a jumping-off point for transatlantic passenger flights, had a more nuanced view of sharing their grazings with aeroplanes.

The area in question, they argued, was their best grazing, and their grazings were already restricted. They feared injury to their cattle if they were grazing when aeroplanes landed. On the last occasion when an aeroplane landed in the district the cattle had stampeded.

'They alleged also that the aeroplanes damaged the grass. Whether it was the rubber tyres or the exhaust fumes they could not say, but the aeroplane which had landed left a reddish track as if the grass had been burnt. The track of the aeroplane which had landed some weeks ago was still visible.

'They had observed the same phenomenon when motor cars and motor cycles crossed the grazings.'

The Land Court agreed to continue hearing the case following a ground inspection. A couple of weeks later, in the middle of July 1934, Midland & Scottish Air Ferries abruptly ceased trading. Its sixteen months of life were enough to establish the venture as the first Scottish civilian airline. Its sudden death opened the door in Lewis to Ted Fresson and Highland Airways.

Captain Fresson never forgot his first approach to the fairway of Melbost Golf Links.

'The markings were clear as I dropped off height,' he wrote later, 'and took a dummy approach and low run over the strip. The smoke wind direction indicator was going strong and the bunker gap, although very narrow, was well marked and looked possible.'

He continued:

There were quite a number of onlookers to witness the first landing on Melbost Golf Course, Lewis. After another circuit we dropped down low over the golf course, motoring in at minimum speed, and touched down almost on top of the first marker. By keeping the tail up I had no difficulty in steering for the middle bunker marker and we ran through the 'bunker straits' without any difficulty, pulling up with fifty yards to spare.

Before going into town, we had a good look round the golf course and I found it had great possibilities for an airfield. I estimated it would cost a few thousand to remove bunkers, and to level and grade four strips of six hundred yards each.

I decided to make a report on the Melbost Golf Course survey and submit it to our next board meeting. Obviously we would need help from the town council to build an airfield in Stornoway in view of the magnitude of the work required. And then there would need to be a good measure of public pressure to obtain the use of the golf course for our purpose.

It would mean extensive alterations to the golf course layout, but I figured we could still retain the eighteen holes. After strolling over the links for an hour, we went into town to the Caledonian Hotel for lunch. Mine host, Kenny Ross, did us proud.

By the time we had finished, it was three o'clock and we were all ready to brave anything which came our way on the flight back.

I changed course for our return trip and made a landfall at Kinlochewe. Dropping down to fifty feet above the water, we flew right down to the east end of

Loch Maree, obtaining a magnificent view, and then pulling up the Glen Docharty pass and down the valley over Achnasheen, Garve, passing Strathpeffer on the left and up the Beauly Firth to Inverness. We landed exactly one hour after take-off from Stornoway.

Just three years later Fresson would fly the same route, from the east coast to the far west of Scotland, in a jaw-dropping thirty-four minutes.

This ground-breaking initiative to link the island of Lewis into what was clearly the travel and communications chain of the immediate future directly affected at least three strong local interest groups.

The crofters of Steinish, Melbost and elsewhere in the neighbourhood had no passionate opinions about air travel one way or the other, but they were interested in the integrity of their grazings.

The meeting of the Stornoway Trust in May 1933, which considered the first approach from Midland & Scottish Air Ferries, 'had before them at the same time a letter from the Free Church Presbytery of Lewis, asking that in the event of a civil aviation company approaching them for a landing ground, the Trustees should give the Presbytery an opportunity of making representations to ensure the preservation of the Lord's Day'. The Trustees 'unanimously agreed to grant the Presbytery's request if occasion should arise'. There would be no civilian flights into or out of Lewis on the Sabbath in the foreseeable future.

Then there were the golfers. Stornowegians and their guests had been playing golf on the links at Melbost since the 1880s. Golf was not perfectly aligned with the traditional crofting use of common grazings and the two exercises sometimes led to squabbles, although only very occasionally to full-scale turf wars. Golfing and crofting had an uneasy relationship throughout the Highlands and Islands. They often shared the land, at least for part of the year, and golf courses offered crofters part-time work as groundsmen and caddies. But the suspicion never disappeared that one was the natural heritor of the turf, and the other was a frivolous latecomer which imperiously laid claim to precious grazings.

Aeroplanes, as the crofters had indicated, could be a threat to both. Even in the light legislative climate of the 1930s, it clearly was not feasible for golfers to enjoy an uninterrupted round while a biplane was coming in to land on the fairway, or for pilots to attempt a landing while pedestrians carrying golf clubs were strolling about on the turf beneath their wheels.

Organised golf had arrived at the Steinish and Melbost machair in the 1880s. The earliest written record was of 1890, when 'the course consists of nine holes – five out and four in – situated on the Melbost links within 3 miles of the Burgh of Stornoway and runs parallel to the shores of Broad Bay stretching out for fully a mile and a half'. The island's future Member of Parliament Dr Donald Murray, who was himself a Stornoway man and was born in 1862, said in a public address to fellow Lewis golfers in the summer of 1913, 'Stornoway Golf Club has been in existence now for over a quarter of a century . . .'

The few early members of Stornoway Golf Club competed on a nine-hole course at Melbost for their first trophy, 'Major Jackson's medal', which was presented to the club by Major Randle Jackson of Swordale in Point, in October 1890. 'The weather was anything but favourable, a strong gusty wind prevailing, making driving difficult, and necessitating very careful judgment at the exposed and wind-swept portions of the course.' The competition was won after 'an exciting finish' with a round of 102 from the Lewis estate chamberlain William MacLennan. It was not recorded whether MacLennan's 102 was achieved over nine or eighteen holes.

'It is not generally known,' reported *The Scotsman* in July 1900, 'that there is a delightful course at the capital of the Lewis':

> The course is situated about three miles from the town, and lies along the southern shore of the famous Broad Bay, between the townships of Steinish and Melbost. The sands along the beach are strewn with innumerable beautiful and large shells. To the north one looks across the bay to the famous cliffs of Gress. For natural beauty and fresh air this golf course cannot be surpassed.
>
> The turf is first-class, and one would need to search for 'scrapes' and bad lies through the green. There is more than enough of links for an eighteen-hole course, although at present there are only nine. The hazards are all natural ones — the usual sand bunkers and a little burn. The sixth hole is a real sporting one, and might be placed amongst the most difficult one-stroke holes.
>
> The tee is on Melbost Point, and you have to drive across the sea on to a green the back of which is guarded by the little burn. A topped shot is sure to land on the beach.
>
> The chief difficulty which the club has to contend with is the lack of members. It is this which prevents them laying out a course of eighteen holes, and also putting the work upon the greens which would make

them perfect. Just now these are simply the natural turf. Certainly this is much better than many made greens, but a little outlay would work a vast improvement.

There are so few playing members it is unnecessary to put up the flags except on Saturdays. Visitors who wish to carry away a pleasant recollection from Stornoway can easily arrange for a game. The principal bookseller will give all information and introduce any one to the members.

In 1891 the crofters, emboldened by the security of tenure given to them by Parliament five years earlier, asserted themselves at Melbost links and attempted to harass and evict the few active golfers from their grazings. The Matheson family intervened as landowners and persuaded the Crofters Commission to oblige the crofters to accept a compensation rental of £7 a year in return for 'the free exercise of the game of golf' on 192 acres of Melbost shoreline.

In the flush of the dawn of the twentieth century, Stornoway Golf Club blossomed. Its membership involved non-playing affiliates as well as golfers, and the spouses and families of both. As the links became busier, the crofters once again became concerned.

In 1912 the Melbost crofters, who wanted the golf course fenced off at the golfers' expense, devised a cunning manoeuvre. In the summer months they removed their cattle from the links. As a natural result the grass grew long. Stornoway Golf Club was unable to mow it, as that would involve an unauthorised harvest of crofting pasturage. The fairways and greens quickly became unplayable. The Scottish Land Court was asked to intervene, and another compromise solution was agreed between all parties at a site meeting on the machair.

In June 1913, one comfortable summer before the cannons began to roar on the western front of An Cogadh Mòr, the great and the good of Edwardian Stornoway gathered at a remarkable event to celebrate and support the town's golf club.

It was billed as a bazaar. It would later be known as a sale of work. It filled Stornoway Town Hall for two full days in early June with almost a hundred women behind stalls selling bric-a-brac, embroidery, baking and refreshments. Its purpose was to raise £450 to build a new golfing clubhouse at Melbost links. Stornoway Golf Club had become an assertion of the burgh's ambitions and identity. As such, the *Press and Journal* reported, it required 'a handsome new pavilion, comprising ladies' and gentlemen's club-rooms, tea rooms, keeper's dwelling house, etc . . . The growing popularity of the game, especially among the ladies, rendered necessary the erection of a more commodious club-house than the one that has served for the past few years.'

Opening the event, Provost John Mackenzie told the gathering that 'Stornoway is possessed of a golf course which is second to none in Scotland, with its natural bunkers and hazards, not to mention its glorious sandy beach . . .

'A few years ago golfers visiting the links had to carry their clubs to and from the course. Such a state of matters could hardly be allowed to continue, and a small house was erected some years ago to meet the then requirements of the game.

'As time went on, however, the membership increased at such a rate that the club found there was no alternative but to face the question of a larger and more commodious golf house. This pavilion when opened will be a credit to the club, and a boon to strangers and townspeople alike . . .'

The ladies raised £500, £50 more than their target. A hundred years later that £500 would be the equivalent of £50,000.

In 1913 it was more than enough to build a handsome new clubhouse on Melbost machair.

Twenty years and a world war later, the golfers of Stornoway found themselves holding an Extraordinary General Meeting to discuss the future not only of their pavilion but also of their links course itself. They heard that 'the Stornoway Trustees might erect a municipal aerodrome beside the fairway, and that the fairway itself might be used a landing ground without interfering with the playing of golf . . .

'At its meeting the Golf Club, while approving wholeheartedly of the suggestion that there should be a municipal aerodrome, unanimously decided against having it on the golf course. It was pointed out that not only one hole would be endangered if the project was on, but the first, fifteenth, sixteenth, seventeenth, and eighteenth.

'The general feeling was that, although at first the aerodrome might not interfere with the playing of golf, as it developed it would ultimately come to be a choice between golf and the aerodrome.'

The concerns of all those parties, which made a uniquely difficult diplomatic path for Edwin Aldred and the Stornoway Trustees to tread, were soon overtaken by world events and rendered irrelevant.

On 2 March 1936 Malcolm K. Macmillan got to his feet in the House of Commons and asked the Under-Secretary of State for Air 'what the present position is regarding the preparation of a landing field at Stornoway, Isle of Lewis; and when a regular air service between the island of Lewis and the mainland will begin?'

Lieutenant-Colonel Anthony Muirhead, a Somerset Conservative MP and the Under-Secretary in question, replied, 'A regular air service cannot be operated until a suitable aerodrome is provided at Stornoway.'

By 'aerodrome', Muirhead meant more than a large aeroplane hangar. He was referring to what would later be described as a small airport, complete with runways and other facilities.

It was not answer enough for Macmillan.

Malcolm Kenneth Macmillan was 22 years old in March 1936, and in his fifth month as Member of Parliament for the Western Isles. He was the oldest son of a Lewis couple, Kenneth Macmillan and Mary Macaulay, who had married in 1903, in Cape Town, South Africa, where Kenneth was working as a mining engineer. Malcolm's older sister Jessie was born in Zimbabwe, which was then named Rhodesia, shortly before the young family returned to Lewis. Once they were back in the island Kenneth set himself up as a building contractor, and Malcolm was born in a house overlooking Stornoway harbour in 1913. From Cape Town, South Africa, to South Beach, Stornoway, by way of Salisbury, Rhodesia, Kenneth and Mary Macmillan kept a Gaelic-speaking household.

A clever and ambitious boy, Malcolm Macmillan left the Nicolson Institute to study law. At the youngest permissible age of 21 years, early in 1935, he was adopted by the Lewis Labour Party as its prospective parliamentary candidate.

Since its inception in 1918 and the days of Donald Murray, the Western Isles had been a Liberal seat. At the General Election of November 1935 it was defended by the Ayrshire man Thomas Ramsay. Malcolm K. Macmillan defeated Ramsay by almost 1,400 votes, or 10 per cent of the small island election turnout, and travelled south from Stornoway to become, at the age of 22, the youngest member of the House of Commons.

Macmillan inherited a plateful of local matters which demanded attention, but throughout the 1930s he chipped away at a succession of government junior ministers on behalf of the Stornoway Trust and its potential airport at Melbost.

Essentially, the Air Ministry refused to issue a civilian flights licence for Melbost airstrip until its runways and other facilities were drastically improved. Neither the Stornoway Trust, as the landowner and main driver of the initiative, nor the Town Council had the money to pay such a bill of works. Macmillan asked if the Air Ministry itself would write a cheque and was stiffly informed that 'it is not the policy of the Government to give assistance in the initial establishment of aerodromes'.

The situation was complicated by the arrival of another aviation entrepreneur promising a seaplane service to and from the east coast of Lewis, which would obviate the need for terrestrial facilities, but that also fell through.

'To cut a long story short,' remembered Ted Fresson,

> bickering over that aerodrome dragged on until four years later, early 1939, before we got the site approved by the owners and golf community.
>
> We could get no local financial support and so Scottish Airways had to finance the construction. It cost us around eight thousand pounds to produce those four runways.
>
> They were not finished until the end of August 1939. The Second World War came on 3rd September and we never used that aerodrome. Our eight thousand pound airfield, unused, was torn up and a large modern airfield was built by the government for the use of Coastal Command.
>
> I believe we obtained compensation from the government for the money we spent to no purpose. It was not until 24 May 1944, towards the end of the War,

that the Air Ministry allowed us to operate the first Inverness–Stornoway service.

So the crofters and golfers continued to co-exist on their links grazings until 1940 when the wartime Air Ministry stepped in, took over the land and built an aerodrome which met their own exacting requirements because it was to be used by the Royal Air Force.

At that point both the grazings and the golf course were effectively obliterated. Coastal Command had no time or use for floral machair land or picturesque fairways. The military built four hard, permanent, tarmacadamed runways, including a long strip running roughly north to south with a couple of east–west branch lines. Ted Fresson made one significant flight between the new landing ground at Melbost and Inverness. Then they all, crofters, golfers, aviators, MPs and members of the Stornoway Trust, settled down to defeating Adolf Hitler's Third Reich.

During the war against totalitarianism it was imperative that local democracy should be asserted at home. Elections to the Stornoway Trust continued, as did the steady, orderly turnover of accountable Trustees.

Ten years after the establishment of the Trust, the decennial anniversary elections of 1934 saw a complete change of personnel in elected Trustees from ten years earlier. Some of that was inevitable. In June 1928 Kenneth Mackenzie, the first chair of the Stornoway Trust and a provost of the town, whose name would be written on the island's tweed industry for the following century, died of tuberculosis at the age of 61 in his home in Matheson Road.

Kenneth Mackenzie was attended at the last by Dr John Tolmie, who had topped the poll at the first Trust elections in

1924. Three years later, in February 1931, Doctor Jack would also be dead, of heart failure at the age of 51 years. Stornoway was a small town requiring endless renewal.

There was a well-attended town hall eve-of-poll hustings before that 1934 election. Several members of the audience asked pointed questions about the Trust's finances. The first flush of community ownership had worn off, the honeymoon period was over, and the unease that was felt at the time about whether Stornoway had bitten off more than it could chew was reflected in the election result.

The blacksmith Ossian Macaskill, who had been a vocal critic of the management of the estate by his fellow Trustees, recommended that the estate 'be placed in the hands of a judicial factor'. He referred to sums of money which he alleged the Trust had spent in litigation. 'It had good assets to begin with,' he announced, 'but they have been blasted out of existence.' The Manor Farm was the only thing left, Mackaskill asserted.

Kenneth MacDonald, who had topped the poll at the previous election, spoke of the great improvement which had been made in the management of the estate within the last three years. When he took office the Manor Farm was yielding the Trust only £8 of profit, but in the previous year its profit was over £900. The profit would have been greater had the Trust not decided to reduce the price of milk to the community in the winter months. The whole herd of cattle on the farm had been improved, said Kenneth MacDonald, who was broadly supported by the other candidates, and practically all the milk supplied was now from tuberculin-tested stock. They looked forward to the day when they would be able to supply Grade A milk.

In the event, just two of the sitting members retained their seats at the 1934 election: the popular Kenneth MacDonald, the only successful candidate from the established status quo, whose personal vote nonetheless fell from 634 to 321, and the critical blacksmith Ossian Macaskill, whose vote held steady. The other three, including Colin Scott Mackenzie, the father of a son of the same name who would become known in Lewis as a solicitor and bailie, were voted out and replaced by William Mackenzie, George MacLeod and Ebenezer Mackenzie.

The newcomers quickly learned that the improvement of the annual accounts was only one part of the Trustees' work. Some social problems, which the Stornoway Trust was duty-bound to tackle, persisted for so long in Lewis that they were almost endemic. Among them was the fate and the future of the landless cottar class which Calum 'Safety' Smith would highlight both in writing and during his time serving on the Trust.

In the twentieth century, cottars were more frequently referred to as squatters. They camped on the edge of townships, living – as Calum Smith knew all too well – a precarious existence. They often reclaimed land and turned rough moor into productive arable. They sometimes built their own family homes. They paid no rent or rates or taxes. They were able to pick up piecework in labouring jobs or even on the fishing fleet. Their children were sent to the nearest local school. But their lives on the margins of Barvas Moor were precarious to the last degree. Squatters and their families could be evicted at any time, upon which they had no legal recourse and no place to go.

It became a principle of the Stornoway Trust to bring those people, several hundred of whom were still living on the estate in the 1930s, in from the cold – to establish them with homes and even some land as responsible and contributing members of island society. Ultimately, with welcome help from the council, that ambition would be realised. But the process was not smooth, and was sometimes beset by hostility from members of the established crofting community.

In most places the Trust's policy 'to rope in all the squatters on the estate, give them allotments of the land they hold, and so regularise their position,' as *The Scotsman* described it, went smoothly. 'Most of the crofters, too, see the advantages of regularising the position, because until that is done there is little hope of a stop being put to fresh squatting.'

But as the sporadic raids on Lewis farms throughout the 1930s suggested, land hunger was still alive and the land wars were within living memory. Crofters who had only recently been given crofts, which applied to many on the Stornoway estate, or who had been offered security of tenure less than fifty years earlier, which applied to all of them, were sensitive to any suggestion of dilution of their rights on their hard-won properties.

A flashpoint arrived at Tolsta, the most northerly township in the estate, in the April of 1936. Large parts of Tolsta had only recently been recrofted. Bordered as it was to the north and west by open moorland, there was a substantial community of upwards of forty squatters around Tolsta's seventy-seven registered crofters.

Relations between the two had often been suspicious and sour. In the middle of April 1936 factor Edwin Aldred made his way up the long road north to measure out the land at Tolsta which the Stornoway Trust intended to resume and then rent out to the neighbourhood's squatters.

When he arrived, Aldred was immediately surrounded by crofters who 'dissuaded' him from continuing. He returned the following day and managed to measure two plots before being once again dissuaded.

On the third day Edwin Aldred went into Tolsta to meet the local grazings committee. By then the national press had been alerted, and *The Scotsman* duly covered events.

> [Aldred] was met in the village by a large crowd of men, some of whom gesticulated wildly and shook their fists.
> He attempted to reason with them, but the men were determined on their point of view. They declared that if any fresh attempt were made to measure the squatters' plots they would seize the ground officer's chain and other instruments. Some of them threatened that military coercion would be necessary to make them submit. After their discussion with the factor the men marched off in a body cheering.
> The Stornoway Trustees discussed the situation, and the general view was that the Tolsta people were under a misapprehension as to the trustees' intentions. They seemed to forget that the trustees could not resume a single plot until the matter had gone before the land court. It was decided to instruct the ground officer to proceed civilly and cautiously, and to advise the people that it would be unwise to interfere with him.

In the following week, amicable discussions between the representatives of all parties resulted in a draft peace proposal which involved everybody swallowing a small measure of compromise. It was offered by the negotiators, ratified by the Trustees and accepted by the crofters.

With war drums beating around Europe, in April 1937 Bailie W.J. Tolmie noted at a meeting of the Stornoway Trust that the people of the south coast of England would probably soon be deserting their homes, which were vulnerable to air raids and invasion. He saw a means of turning a threat into an opportunity. 'The Hebrides are the safest place in Britain,' said Bailie Tolmie, 'and the trust should offer building sites . . . in the neighbourhood of Stornoway excellent sites could be offered.'

On that occasion Bailie Tolmie's advice was not taken by his fellow Trustees or by the Town Council. That was to prove wise, for when the war came most people experienced more difficulties getting in and out of the Hebrides than had been the case since the Middle Ages.

Shortly after the declaration of war on Nazi Germany on 3 September 1939, most of the north and west of Scotland became a restricted travel zone. Wary of enemy agents or worse landing surreptitiously in the lonely islands and deep sea lochs, the government required people travelling to and from the Hebrides to obtain specially prepared photo passes, identification cards separate from the traditional passport, and transportation by land and sea, even between islands, was monitored.

The new regime caused some consternation in Inverness, which was most people's entrepôt to the northern Highlands and Islands. Seven months after the outbreak of the second great war of the twentieth century, in March 1940, the long-serving Inverness town clerk James Cameron said that with leisure travel overseas so strictly limited, the Highlands, which in 1939 had attracted no fewer than 22,000 hikers, could ordinarily expect a bumper season but for 'the virtual closing of this area of Scotland to tourist traffic'.

'At present,' explained Mr Cameron, 'it takes about ten to twelve days to obtain a permit to enter the area. Representation should go forward from the Council to the War Office suggesting that an easier method is evolved for entering the area. It might be that the National Registration Officer of the district could issue special holiday permits obtainable within hours.'

Over in Stornoway, which had not much of a tourist season at the best of times, such matters were of little concern. The golf club's links at Melbost were finally appropriated by the Air Ministry for military purposes. Planes took off from there to guard the Western Approaches and hunt for U-boats. The construction of the hard runways were of short-term as well as long-term benefit to Lewis: as landowners the Stornoway Trust owned the mineral rights on its estate, and received a royalty of three pennies for every cubic ton of aggregate which was quarried to pave over the land at Melbost links. Later in the war the aerodrome at Melbost became a gateway for United States personnel to land in Britain.

Lews Castle was requisitioned by the Admiralty, along with its gardens, outhouses, boat house, slipway and adjacent land. The building was deployed as a naval hospital, its grounds were deployed as training areas, and its grander rooms became mess halls for Royal Navy and Royal Air Force officers berthed in the town, who occasionally had to share the place with enemy prisoners of war. Compensation of £7,055 for those intrusions was agreed with the Stornoway Trust in 1949 and paid in 1950. The Trustees were at least as grateful for the fact that during the five years of requisition, the Admiralty shouldered the burden of care and maintenance of Lews Castle.

Not all domestic interests were shelved for the duration. In the summer of 1941 the formidable and much-loved minister of Stornoway Free Church of Scotland, Kenneth A. MacRae, was alarmed by being told that 'the RAF were playing football on Sabbath on the Melbost pitch'. He promptly wrote to the commanding officer of RAF Stornoway 'and asked him to act as the naval authorities have done in prohibiting games on the Sabbath'.

The commanding officer replied, pointing to the arduous wartime duties facing his men and their need for recreation, but agreeing that there would be no more 'Sunday games'. Reverend MacRae suggested that 'the men might more profitably use up their surplus energies by walking into the church services in Stornoway'.

Two years later, in the October of 1943, members of the Free Church congregation were 'surprised and hurt' when, on their way to church one Sunday, they saw 'a reaper at work in one of the fields of the Manor Farm'. By 'a reaper' they did not mean a lone man or woman with a scythe, although he or she would also have been unacceptable. They meant that they had seen and heard a large and discordant piece of agricultural machinery. Kenneth A. MacRae was once again forced reluctantly into action, writing to the farm's manager William Duncan, the Minister for Agriculture in London, and the Stornoway Trust as owners of the farm.

William Duncan responded that the Sabbath day in question 'was the only really good day we had for a week. I do not go out to harvest to be a nuisance to anyone. I go for the benefit of the people of Stornoway and for the benefit of the animals on the farm. Had I not got that corn on the Sunday it would have gone to rot. I come from Angus, and people there are working seven days in the week in the production of food. The machinery made no more noise than cars and buses on the highway.'

William Duncan was, however, no longer in Angus. Work on the Sabbath day, with machinery or by hand, continued to be prohibited on Stornoway Trust property.

The Second World War in Europe ended in May 1945 and the serving men and women slowly returned to their eternal Lewis, finding to their relief a civilisation largely unchanged by the conflict.

Some traditions died harder than others. In December 1945 eleven returned servicemen raided land at Melbost aerodrome and staked out house sites. The men had no need to copy the actions of their fathers after the First World War, said the chair of the Stornoway Trust, Provost A.J. Mackenzie. They lived in different times. 'The trustees will be quite ready to provide housing sites for as many ex-servicemen as possible, provided it is done in an orderly manner and for the good of all.'

The raids had actually been predicted to Trustees by their factor Edwin Aldred, who reported earlier in 1945, 'The provision of land as a precursor to the provision of houses for returning ex-servicemen is an alternative to possible raiding of farm lands and has been causing me some concern during recent months.'

As a result, before the raid the Stornoway Trust had decided to make available to the Town Council a seven-acre field in which to erect housing at Laxdale, and to offer the Board of Agriculture plots of land for new crofts. It stood in stark contrast to the response of the landowner after the previous war, but severe land hunger took a great deal of time to assuage. As late as 1950 there were still seventeen squatters in the grounds of Lews Castle. With a will, however, that land hunger could and would be satisfied.

7

Not a Land Problem, But a Housing One

Both locally and nationally, the Second World War killed far fewer soldiers, sailors and air crew than had the First World War.

The United Kingdom as a whole lost 383,600 military personnel between 1939 and 1945, which amounted to less than half of the 886,000 First World War casualties. The Second World War took 34,000 Scottish service people, after 134,000 had lost their lives in the First.

In the island of Lewis, the crippling burden of over 1,000 dead in the First World War fell to 297 in the Second World War.

No single death was any easier to bear, a world entire disappeared with each mortality, but at least the Hebrides were spared the large increase in Second World War civilian casualties caused in the mainland of the United Kingdom and in the rest of Europe by urban bombing and state sponsored mass-murder.

For the most obvious of reasons there had been no national census in 1941. The survey of 1951 was therefore the first since devastating crashes in the Lewis population had been revealed in 1921 and 1931.

It confirmed what most other Hebrideans knew from first-hand experience, that their archipelago was suffering from a long, drawn-out decline. The consolation for Lewis was that the biggest island's diminution was less severe than others. Across the Minch in Skye, for example, the population of the second-biggest British offshore island contracted by fully 14 per cent between 1931 and 1951. In the same period the larger population of Lewis fell by 6 per cent, from 25,205 to 23,731 people. It was still worrying, but not a time for panic.

The war years had been a hiatus from which, in 1945 and 1946, people had to emerge and resume normality. The large and small issues and challenges facing bodies such as the Stornoway Trust had not disappeared. They had been on ice, and in 1945 they were removed gingerly from the deep freeze and allowed to thaw.

A civilian air service between the Scottish mainland and Melbost links was finally permitted by the Air Ministry and inaugurated in May 1944, by which time the military imperative to patrol the Western Approaches was not as great as it had been earlier in the war, the skies over Scotland were relatively safe, and the Royal Air Force was reducing its presence in Stornoway. The first itineraries followed a precedent set briefly in 1940, by flying from Renfrew in the Central Belt to Stornoway via Tiree and occasionally also North Uist. The longest such journey on de Havilland *Rapide* eight-passenger biplanes, which were constructed largely from plywood, took four hours and twenty-five minutes between Scotland and Lewis, with the return flight leaving Melbost on the following morning. That Lowland service set the tone for future flights to and from Lewis, and for the rest of the western islands. In Inverness, RAF Dalcross, which like Melbost had been built and operated as a military airport during the Second World

War, replaced the Longman airstrip as the town's civilian airport in 1947. Ted Fresson, who lived there, and his colleagues ensured a service from Inverness to the northern islands of Orkney and Shetland from the earliest days, but commercial flights from Inverness to the Outer Hebrides were included only as part of the Renfrew–Stornoway service. Between 1947 and 1973 the national carrier British Airways flew aeroplanes six days a week on a wide loop between Glasgow, Benbecula, Stornoway and Inverness. On the seventh day the de Havillands and their pilots rested, for it was the Sabbath day.

In June 1945, with Adolf Hitler defeated and dead, the Stornoway Trust began the tortuous process of claiming compensation from the Air Ministry for their annexation of Melbost links four years earlier.

The Trust was not alone. Sitting in Stornoway, the Land Court heard representations from the Stornoway Trust, the tenant of Melbost Farm, Stornoway Golf Club, and 'a large number of crofters in Melbost, Branahuie, Steinish, and Sandwick'. Those claimants were requesting the four members of the Land Court to tell the Air Ministry to award them a total of £35,000.

Particular interest was taken in the golf club's submission. Stornoway golfers were among the least likely of Leòdhasaich to resent contributions to the war effort. But more than any other group, they had been put out of hearth and home. With Melbost links operating as a civilian commercial airport there was no prospect of them returning to their old course and clubhouse, so a new one must be found, manicured and equipped.

The Stornoway Trust asked the Land Court to order the Air Ministry to pay £7,500 for the reinstatement of the golf course and £4,300 for the reinstatement of the buildings belonging to the club, 'which were erected on ground belonging to the Stornoway Trustees'.

On behalf of the Trustees, the advocate J.A. Crawford said that 'the provision of recreational facilities is one of the purposes for which the Stornoway Trust exists, and it has been proved that there is a bona-fide intention on the part of the Trustees to devote any compensation granted under that head to the provision of a golf course elsewhere'.

In evidence in support of the Trustees, Bailie Lees said that the loss of the golf course was a serious matter for Stornoway. It was the only recreation available for townsfolk, he said, and visitors had been in the habit of coming to Stornoway for the purpose of playing golf.

Speaking for the Air Ministry, Sir Norman Macpherson submitted that the Stornoway Trustees were entitled to compensation only on the value of the ground and buildings taken. The sums of £7,500 and £4,300 were excessive, said Sir Norman, while stressing, 'In regard to all the claims, my instructions are not to beat the claims down but to leave it to the court to fix a fair compensation.' It was said that the Ministry always drove a hard bargain, but that was not the spirit, he insisted, in which he made his submissions to the Land Court.

In the event, rather than the total of £11,800 claimed by the Stornoway Trust on behalf of the town's golf club, the court awarded £9,600 towards building a new eighteen-hole course and clubhouse.

With the help of factor Edwin Aldred, which the golfers fully acknowledged in their own history of events, 'The Trust had indicated that they intended to allot ground within the Castle Policies as the site for the new course, and although there were suggestions that alternative sites at Vatisker and

NOT A LAND PROBLEM, BUT A HOUSING ONE

Barvas be considered – nostalgia perhaps for a links course – they were discounted as being too remote from Stornoway to attract a sufficient membership.

'The Trust then empowered the new committee to enter into negotiations for the construction of an 18 hole course, the cost not to exceed £6,500. The contract was awarded to John R. Stutt of Paisley. Construction commenced in July 1946 and completed in October 1947 . . . The balance of the compensation award had been set aside for the construction of a clubhouse and 1953 saw the building completed.'

The golf club's new home was therefore placed in the middle of town in the castle grounds, where it remained, although the course and clubhouse would both change dramatically in the succeeding years.

The Western Isles contributed to the 1945 landslide election victory of Clement Attlee's Labour Party by re-electing Malcolm K. Macmillan, who was recently demobbed from the army, with the biggest majority of his young career. The island of Lewis was rewarded in January 1946 with a three-day fact-finding mission from the Under-Secretary of State for Scotland.

Tom Fraser was a 35-year-old former coal miner and union official who had been the Member of Parliament for Hamilton in Lanarkshire since the seat was vacated in 1943. It was Fraser's first visit to the Outer Hebrides, and he flew to Stornoway from Renfrew in seventy-five minutes, causing one observer to wonder if 'he may have found it rather more difficult than some of his predecessors to appreciate the remoteness of the Hebrides from the Scottish Office'.

Once on the ground Fraser, accompanied by officials from the departments of Agriculture and Health, wasted no time in going to see the chair of the Stornoway Trust, provost of

Stornoway, and vice-convener of Ross & Cromarty County Council, A.J. Mackenzie, to discuss land raids and housing requirements.

At the end of the third day Tom Fraser admitted, 'I do not know whether I have covered all the problems of Lewis during my visit, but I have certainly covered a great many of them. Some of them I have covered over and over again, and it has interested me to find different people reaching the same conclusions for different reasons.'

As well as Stornoway, the Under-Secretary visited Point, Tolsta, Ness and North Lochs, meeting with crofters as well as elected representatives and businessmen. His principal interest, said Fraser, was in land and housing, and he 'discussed these questions at considerable length with the chairman and factor of the Stornoway Trust', the chairman and secretary of the Agricultural Executive Committee, and a deputation from the Lewis branch of the British Legion, which had supported the Sandwick and Melbost land raiders a few months earlier. The British Legion deputation included a number of ex-servicemen from different parts of the island, who advised Tom Fraser of their problems locally. Fraser said afterwards, 'It has been represented by some of those whom I have met that, so far as the immediate vicinity of Stornoway is concerned, the problem I have to investigate is not a land problem, but a housing one.

'In the rural areas,' he said, 'schemes of land settlement may have been found necessary, but also it has been represented to me that many of the returning servicemen who are desirous of procuring holdings are chiefly concerned with the provision of houses.'

Tom Fraser, and the Stornoway Trustees and councillors who were advising him, were right. Much of the clamour for crofts which followed both world wars, and dominated a lot

Left. William Hesketh Lever, Viscount Leverhulme of the Western Isles.
(Chronicle/Alamy Stock Photo)

Below. Town and country: crofters in the 1970s drive sheep home to Point from the Stornoway General Pasture.

The rebuilt Stornoway Town Hall in 1929. The first Stornoway Trust offices were on the ground floor.

Provost Kenneth Mackenzie, the first chair of the Stornoway Trust. (Stornoway Historical Society)

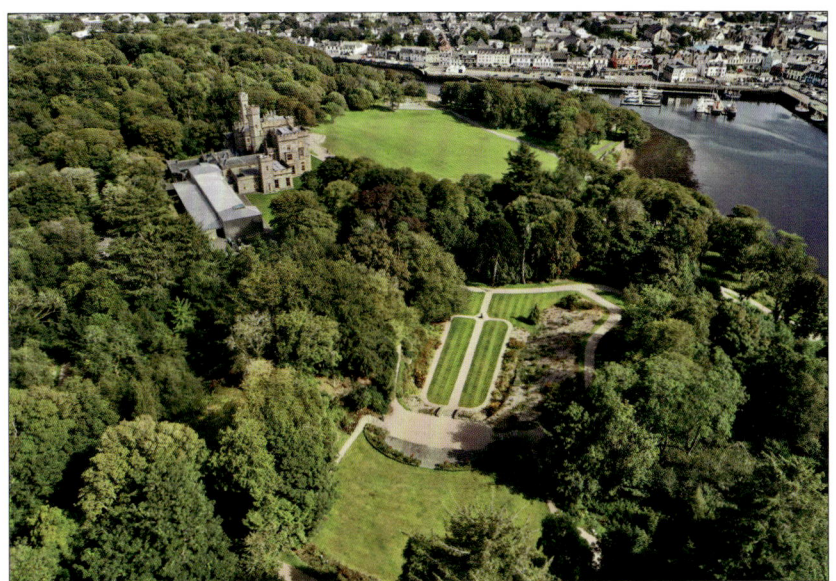

Lews Castle and the sunken garden, looking north over the town to Broad Bay. (Chris Murray)

Eastward over Stornoway towards Melbost, the airport and the crofting lands of Point. (Chris Murray)

A crofting family making hay in Back, *c.*1950s. (Back Historical Society)

Taking in the hay, Back, *c.*1950s. (Back Historical Society)

Sheep-dipping in Gress, *c.*1950s. (Back Historical Society)

Thatching in Coll, *c*.1950s. (Back Historical Society)

A rich man's playground: Lews Castle with arboretum and tennis court in its Edwardian pomp, before the Trust inherited the building and policies.

Lews Castle in the twenty-first century.

The Porters' Lodge: the original gateway to the castle.

The Hebridean Celtic – HebCelt – festival on the castle green in 2022.

Edwin Aldred, Stornoway Trust estate factor, 1928–61.

D. M. Smith, Stornoway Trust estate factor, 1961–93.

Trustees following the 1994 elections: (back row) Iain M. Maciver (Factor), Neil M. Graham, D. H. M. Maciver, Alexander (Sandy) Matheson, Iain A. Macleod (Chairman), Malcolm Macfarlane; (front row) Roderick J. Murray, Kenneth A. Maciver, Charles B. Nicolson, Angus Macleod, Neil Macdonald.

The Drillmaster oil rig tied up at Arnish in the 1970s.

Arnish in the late 1970s, with the accommodation ship for visiting contract workers.

Trainee welders at their booths at Arnish in the 1970s. (Stornoway Historical Society)

Four of the last provosts of Stornoway, who were also ex-officio chairs of the trust: Alexander (Sandy) Matheson (b. 1941; Provost 1972–75); Alexander John (Alasdair) Mackenzie (1894–81; Provost 1939–59); Ann Urquhart (1901–87; Provost 1965–68); Donald James Stewart (1920–92; Provost 1959–65 and 1968–70. (Stornoway Historical Society)

Marybank Quarry, owned by the Stornoway Trust and operated by Breeden Hebrides.

Past and present Trustees gathered at the 75th anniversary dinner of the Stornoway Trust in 1999: (back row) Angus Macleod, Kenneth A. Maciver, Neil Macdonald, Murdo Macleod, Alexander (Sandy) Matheson, Donald J. MacSween, Donald J. Macphail, Neil M. Graham; (front row) D. H. M. Maciver, Malcolm Macfarlane, Kenneth Nicolson, Iain A. Macleod (Chairman) Alasdair (Ray) M. Mackenzie, Charles B. Nicolson.

Sawmill workshop under construction in the 1990s.

Blowing in the wind: a wind turbine and a shieling hut on the summer grazings.

Above. A montage of the projected Stornoway Wind Farm.

Left. Iain MacLennan Maciver, Stornoway Estate factor, 1993–present.

Stornoway Trustees in 2023: (left to right) Catriona Murray, Donald F. Crichton, Murdo F. Macleod, Donald I. Nicholson, Marisa Macdonald, Calum Maclean, Calum M. Macdonald, Iain M. Maciver (Factor), Norman A. Maciver (Chairman).

of the peacetime in between, was driven by a simple desire for roofs and hearths. Crofts were coterminous with housing. Many Leòdhasaich also wanted a patch of arable land and a share in grazings. But some, particularly in the neighbourhood of Stornoway, would be perfectly content with decent homes in which to raise their families.

The Stornoway Trust and Stornoway Town Council had cooperated with Ross & Cromarty Council in the 1930s to provide pioneering council-house schemes in Lewis. The scheme at what was known as Manor Park offered a perfect illustration of the friendly, collaborative rivalry which obtained between the Stornoway Trust and Stornoway Town Council, on account of the Trustees and councillors being lifelong acquaintances, colleagues and very often the same people.

When the extensive scheme of fifty-six municipal houses was first mooted early in 1937, the Stornoway Trust happily consented to sell the land north of the town centre to Stornoway Town Council for £12 an acre. The council agreed and all was underway, before the district valuer stepped in to inform all parties that his estimation put the future Assaye Place and Canada Crescent at only £5 an acre.

A deadlock occurred. Three times the Trust offered the council a reduced price; three times it was accepted by the councillors; three times the district valuer insisted that the price was still too high and the deal was rejected by the central arbitrators at the Department of Health on the grounds that it was in excess of the district valuer's assessment. The Department asked for the matter to be settled by arbitration. Both the Trust and the Town Council were anxious to avoid the cost of that procedure.

It was complicated by the fact that six of the nine Stornoway councillors were also members of the Stornoway Trust, and

Provost Roddy Smith was chair of both bodies. 'A majority of the members of both bodies have divided loyalties,' wrote one observer in the Glasgow *Herald*. 'They are proprietors in one capacity, and feuars in another. The Trust is in need of all the money it can get, and so the Trustees are anxious to make the best bargain they can. The Council are anxious to do the same.'

The matter dragged on into the summer of 1937, when, with no price having been agreed, the architect and Town Council workmen began pegging out the house sites. At a subsequent meeting of the Stornoway Trust, Provost Roddy Smith, wearing his Trustee's hat, protested light-heartedly that this was no better than a land raid: the council had taken illegal possession of the Trust's property, like a group of servicemen in the night. Other Trustee/councillors argued in return that the council had acted properly, as the Trust had already agreed to hand over the land and only the price was in dispute. Suggestions that the only three councillors who were not Trustees should decide the matter were rejected by all the others. It was finally agreed to everybody's satisfaction that the sum of £8 an acre should be paid. The scheme opened its doors in 1939.

Following the visit of the Scottish Office Under-Secretary Tom Fraser in January 1946, fifty prefabs were delivered to Stornoway. Prefabricated cottage homes were conceived and executed by the British coalition government as a temporary solution to the wartime housing crisis which had been exacerbated by the German bombing raids which destroyed 200,000 British homes, and the shortage during the first civilian international conflict of builders and their materials. During the Second World War, rather than new houses being raised at however unsatisfactory a pace, existing houses were levelled.

It was originally planned to make and distribute 500,000 prefabs within five years of the end of the war. They were supposed to last for ten years. In the event, 156,623 were constructed before the programme ended in 1951, and a few were still occupied seventy years later, in the third decade of the twenty-first century. Those survivors included some of the fifty which were erected in 1947 in facing rows on Stornoway Trust land at Plasterfield, a mile to the east of the centre of town. Financed and built by the central state, they were very quickly devolved to local authorities, becoming part of the housing stock first of Stornoway Town Council and then of Comhairle nan Eilean (the Western Isles Council) before right-to-buy legislation in the 1980s took them into private hands.

A thriving subculture developed around prefabs in the post-war years, fuelled in part by the fact that they were built from the base materials of wood, concrete, steel and asbestos to two dozen different and unique designs. Like trainspotters, prefab hobbyists would circumnavigate the country in search of examples of the different designs. The homes built outside Stornoway, which would resist the winter blasts from the Atlantic Ocean and the Minch, were known as the 'Isle of Lewis' models. To the occasional bemusement of their inhabitants, they became celebrated in the subculture.

One of the reasons for the shortfall in prefab construction in the second half of the 1940s was the newly elected Labour government's preference for building from bricks and mortar more permanent municipal estates, or council housing. That commitment was realised in the constituency of the Stornoway Trust as much as in Glasgow or London. In 1946 the Town Council announced an ambitious plan to build eighty houses on Macaulay Road, near to the Manor Park scheme.

The unprecedented size of that proposal was indicated by the fact that early in 1947 the Department of Health published its guidelines and limits on new building in that year in Stornoway. The town was restricted to forty new-builds. In any previous twelve months that would have been deemed more than sufficient and would have excited no controversy. During the post-war building boom, it provoked Stornoway Town Council to protest that forty new houses would be insufficient. 'The Council have 80 houses at present building,' it announced. 'There are seven private houses being built in the burgh, and, as 18 Council houses have already been completed this year it is feared that the nominal 40 really represents only 15 more Council houses in 1947.' The limit was increased.

In July 1947 the Stornoway Trust declared, with a certain pride, that its previous fiscal year had turned a profit of £1,600. That allowed the Trustees to reserve £1,000 in a contingency fund, and invest the other £600 in 'social and charitable purposes'. The Trust was 'investigating the possibilities of [land] reclamation and afforestation in the Parish of Stornoway', with a view to submitting a scheme to the advisory panel of that precursor of the Highlands and Islands Development Board, the Highlands and Islands Development Commission.

Factor Edwin Aldred was asked by the Trustees to investigate possible schemes and report back. Aldred enlisted the Hurd and Schmidt consultancy, and their report noted in 1947 that 'the main island industries were weaving and herring fishing'. There had been an increase in spinning mills, remodelling of existing mills and the possibility of further expansion due to the harbour development programme. To support non-crofting employment, new industrial zoning was proposed.

The report also reviewed housing and social amenities in Stornoway. While new accommodation was needed to resolve the housing shortage and overcrowding, and residential zoning should primarily be residential, it was proposed, sensitive to traditional Lewis family-based economic activity, that this might include a group of outhouses for weaving, poultry keeping or some form of handicraft.

As for the Castle grounds, the consultants suggested that they could be used as a plant nursery to supply trees for shelter belts in the villages throughout Lewis.

In the summation of Helen Haugh, the consultants anticipated increased tourism and when modernising Stornoway, they cautioned the Trustees to ensure that 'the greatest vigilance is maintained and reasonable regard' be made to the 'traditional character of the older streets' because 'tourists appreciate well-kept traditional Scottish architecture'.

Consistent with the aims of the Trust, and mindful of the lack of social venues in Stornoway, the consultants proposed the construction of a community centre with restaurant and cloak rooms (for those in transit to or from the country areas), a large hall (seating for 1,000) for concerts, films and theatre, a lesser hall, reading and news rooms, billiard and committee rooms, and possibly a gymnasium and swimming pool: 'The community centre would serve as a central point from which village halls in other parts of the island could derive help, particularly as a distribution centre for films, entertainments and exhibitions and possibly for the library service.'

In 2021 Helen Haugh, an associate professor in Community Enterprise at the Cambridge Judge Business School, University of Cambridge, prepared a report on the functioning of the Stornoway Trust between 1923 and 1960, titled 'Becoming Sustainable'.

Professor Haugh divided those four decades into three phases. They were, broadly speaking, the period following its establishment in 1923, when the first Trustees assessed how much or how little they had been given, and what they might and might not do with their unexpected power and influence.

There were then the hungry 1930s, during which they shook the Stornoway Trust into profit without betraying its founding principles, and following which decade they found themselves immersed in another international war. Only in the post-war era of the late 1940s and 1950s was a new generation of Trustees given the time and space and security to look around and plan imaginatively for the future.

As well as apparently insatiable land hunger and need for housing, Haugh noted that the new landlords of eastern Lewis had to deal with the collapse of the local fishing fleet as a cornerstone employer. As most of the Lewis boats worked out of Stornoway, those statistics had an especially grim effect on the Trust's own constituents.

The fact that the Trustees were able to operate at all, and that they kept on going, was remarkable. 'In the first few years of the Trust,' notes Helen Haugh, 'the finances were precarious, and a surplus was not made until 1933. Although the Trust owned land and property, there was little cash or revenue with which to administer the estate. Between 31.12.1924 and 31.12.38 the value of heritable property held by the Trust falls from £26,905 to £21,598 . . .'

An idea of the contortions, nerve and conviction which were required in those years to keep the Stornoway Trust afloat is offered by Professor Haugh's matter-of-fact summary of the ledgers. Firstly, the 'assets' which had been so generously gifted by Leverhulme flattered to deceive. They were often in the red, rarely profitable, and occasionally ruinously expensive to operate. It dawned on the Trustees that the Island of Lewis estate, to which Stornoway was central, had been calibrated not as a hard-headed business, but as the plaything of a couple of the richest men on earth, James Matheson and William Hesketh Lever. Its function was not to make money – neither of them needed more money when they bought Lewis – but to indulge their different fantasies.

The Lewis Dairy Farmers Association Ltd (LDFA) was the name given by Leverhulme to the dairy that he established on Scotland Street to act as a middleman between the cattle farms and the customers. Its shares were gifted to the Trust, along with those of the Stornoway Gas Company, Stornoway Fish Products and the Lewis Steam Laundry. The latter was also established by Leverhulme when he was told that the Stornoway bourgeoisie was obliged to send its dirty washing across the breadth of Scotland to Inverness. Not one of those enterprises showed more than a negligible profit and all of them were either sold off or closed down by the Trustees within a few years.

'Between 1923 and 1938,' writes Helen Haugh,

> the two principal income sources are first, income from land, house rents, feu duties, farms, and shooting and fishing. Income from land, house rents and feu duties for the first trading period ending 31.12.1924 was £4,946 and increased by small increments each year to £5,123 on 31.12.1938. Annual rent collections were gathered at sites across estate land. In addition to land rent, tenants paid a feu duty to the Trust as superior and freeholder. The feu duty was paid twice a year, usually in arrears, on Whitsunday (15 May) and Martinmas (11 November). Feu duties increased from £919 in 1924 to £1,430 in 1938.
>
> Located north-east of Stornoway and featured in Leverhulme's milk supply development plans, Manor Farm was included in the estate gifted to the Trust. The book value of Manor Farm increased slowly

between 31.12.1924 (£3,324) and 31.12.38 (£2,892) but operated at a deficit 31.12.1924 (£974) and 31.12.1925 (£76).

The Trust estate earned income from leasing the shooting and fishing estates at Home [south of the Barvas road] and Gress. A small but regular income from shooting and fishing commences in 31.12.1924 (£84) but in the same year incurs costs of £994. Field sports were primarily associated with visitors to Lewis – agreements to lease were managed by an agent – and between 1924 and 1931 the shooting and fishing facilities were profitable . . .

In 1932 a letter from LDFA informs the Trustees that the LDFA had appointed a liquidator, the factor, and that they will cease to pay the £24 per annum for the secretary's salary. The committee unanimously decide to recommend to the Trust that 'the committee came to the conclusion that we do not send any more milk to the dairy after 31.03.32 and that steps be taken to wind up the dairy as soon as possible'. Donald Macleod acquires the dairy premises on Scotland Street and submits an offer of £85 to extend the premises occupied by the dairy buildings, purchased by him. His offer is accepted, and the Trust receives a feu duty of £12 per annum . . .

The laundry was put up for sale, as a going concern, in 1928. Although an offer was received, the laundry was not sold until 1935.

The shares in the Stornoway Gas Company to Trust comprise 3,997 ordinary shares at £1 each (fully paid) at par £3,997, and 430 preference shares of £1 each (fully paid) £430.00; total £4,427.00. The shares earn a modest income . . .

NOT A LAND PROBLEM, BUT A HOUSING ONE

The miracle was not that the Stornoway Trust emerged from all of that as a stable, profitable and responsible social landowner, but that it emerged at all. The pride and determination of Lewis people had to engage fully with their acuity and energy to ensure that a vitally important flagship did not capsize and sink.

In similar circumstances, a second wave of Scottish Highland democratic community landowners in the 1990s and 2000s could expect to receive substantial financial aid and advice from a sympathetic state. In the 1920s and 1930s, not a penny, not a helpful word, nor much sympathy from certain governments, was allowed to the Stornoway Trust.

Only after twenty years and another world war – two decades that would have broken lesser people – could the Trustees clear their heads and look properly to the future. 'The period between 1947 and 1960 marks the Trust's post-WW2 support for the reconstruction of Stornoway town and employment creation projects,' writes Helen Haugh. The Trustees found themselves not only able to bankroll smaller community projects in Back and elsewhere, but also able to extend their remit 'beyond the [Stornoway] estate as the economy of Stornoway is "so closely integrated with that of the whole island", the development of Stornoway could not be considered separately from the island.'

While looking north, west and south to the rest of Lewis, the Trustees of the early 1950s could not help but notice that while much of the obstructive undergrowth had been cleared away, one very large and expensive white elephant still stood in their path.

They then devised a perfect solution, which would simultaneously pass responsibility for the elephant to other hands, while gainfully employing it in a sector which fitted seamlessly into the Stornoway Trust's own manifesto.

On a September day in 1953, Alec Douglas-Home, 14th Earl of Home, a future prime minister who was then a junior minister at the Scottish Office, flew north to Stornoway and made his way to Lews Castle. Once there, Home conducted the official opening of what some southern newspapers described as 'a crofters' university'.

The vocational polytechnic of Lews Castle College had been operating with eighty-five students and nine tutors since the beginning of the month. Most of the students were day pupils but thirty-five of them were boarders, Lewis teenagers from the outlying townships, living, sleeping and learning in the rooms once occupied by Viscount Leverhulme and his family and friends. A visionary collaboration between Ross & Cromarty County Council, into whose education department it fell, the Scottish Office and the Stornoway Trust, Lews Castle College, said Alec Douglas-Home, represented 'the belief that the life of the islands is capable of development'.

'To anybody who is prepared to give serious thought to the future of the Highlands,' the minister continued, 'it should be plain by this time that the islands cannot be preserved as "period pieces". And even if they could, what man or woman who boasted the name of Highlander would wish to live on a reservation as a picturesque survival of a doomed race for the benefit of tourists? If the Highlands are to prosper they must welcome the new ways of looking at life and adapt them to their circumstances. They must encourage their own young people to keep abreast of the times.

'It has been alleged that educational policy has been an important factor in Highland depopulation. Boys and girls of ability have had to leave home for higher education and they tend to stay away. This, of course, from the point of view of Highland prosperity, is suicidal. If the Highlands are ever to be prosperous, the prosperity must be brought to them by Highlanders. Lews Castle College is a first step in that direction. For here the children will get their education on the spot, instead of hundreds of miles away.

'Courses relating to local needs, seafaring, and building will occupy a prominent place in the curriculum. But in addition, Lews Castle marks an important advance in that it will provide full-time and part-time courses of technical education to boys in the 15 to 18 age groups in nautical subjects, textiles and building. It goes without saying that the success of this experiment will depend upon the support it gets from industry.

'It would have been difficult to have made a start,' concluded Lord Home, 'but for the help we have received from the Stornoway Trust in making the castle available for this purpose. It will surely play an invaluable part in preserving and developing all that is best in the old Celtic culture, crafts and pursuits.'

The college's initial courses, as the minister inferred, reflected the occupations of the island, with a notable emphasis on Harris tweed. Chemistry lessons focused on the use of dyes in textiles; art lessons on patterns and design.

Although the building was ultimately unsuitable for a modern college's tuition and residential needs and both students and tutors moved out to purpose-built blocks in the castle grounds, the name of Lews Castle was stamped on the college throughout its growth into a valuable part of an actual Highland university which awarded actual degrees. By the year 2012, Lews Castle College had 2,700 students, representing nine different nationalities, enrolled in 150 full-time, part-time and online courses ranging from archaeology to art and professional cookery to construction and engineering. It had satellite buildings in the southern islands of Benbecula and Barra. It employed 130 staff. In any and all of its manifestations, Lews Castle College directly satisfied a founding ambition of the Stornoway Trustees to foster education in the island of Lewis.

Some of those Trustees, it should be said, might have been more relieved at finally getting rid of the white elephant than made joyful by the introduction of tertiary education to Stornoway. Once the mansion had been passed on to the local government authority, it remained with the local government authority. The Stornoway Trust would not insist on its return.

8

A New Party and a New Council

The Stornoway Trust's 1960s began with the appointment of a new factor. Edwin Aldred retired in 1961. It would require a big person to fill Aldred's boots. The Trustees found that person in D.M. Smith.

Donald Murdo 'D.M.' Smith was a younger brother of the memoirist, newspaper columnist and Stornoway Trustee Calum 'Safety' Smith. He was a Lewisman who was younger than the Trust itself. He had been born in 1928 and raised in its embrace, and had worked for Edwin Aldred for five years before stepping into Aldred's job as factor. That familiarity with the concept of the Trust, and democratic community ownership, would naturally become commonplace with the passage of time. Whole generations of Leòdhasaich would grow up without a first-hand comprehension of their mainland Highland cousins' agitation for 'land reform'. Having known nothing but reformed land ownership, the notion of private absentee landowners was not quite foreign to them – there were several of them in the rest of Lewis – but it was not as pressing as it was in Eigg or Assynt.

Shortly before his own retirement, D.M. Smith summarised the contribution of the Trust to the national debate: 'It is not so much that the Stornoway Trust is a massive local employer,' he said in 1988, 'or a great investor of outside capital into its area – it has little enough land outside crofting to go too far in that direction and is as happy as its crofters with that state of affairs. It is more that the Trust is a body committed at its very heart to a responsible and unexploitative use of its powers as a landlord whether in ploughing small profits quietly back into local improvements and employment schemes, or in dealing with Dutch oil companies.

'If Leverhulme's own plans were insensitively conceived and autocratically announced, he has through his legacy to Lewis left a style of crofting estate management which is the opposite of those things. The Stornoway Trust is unique because it is a guide to nationalisation at local level, without the involvement of the Secretary of State. It is there as a model for a system of community ownership of crofting lands.'

In the 1950s and 1960s the spinning, weaving and tailoring of Harris tweed supplanted saltwater fishing as the main industry in both the town of Stornoway and the country crofting districts of Lewis. The number of resident fishermen in the island fell from 3,425 in 1901, to 2,000 in 1931, and to 432 in 1961.

By the 1960s Stornoway's mills – which had not existed in the previous century – had grown to employ over 1,000 workers in their factory premises and hired another 1,000 freelance pieceworkers at looms in small sheds at the sides of their houses throughout the islands of Lewis and Harris.

Donald Stewart epitomised that journey. Donald James Stewart was born in modest circumstances in Stornoway in 1920, the son of Neil, a 27-year-old drift-net fisherman of the town, and Jessie Mary, his 26-year-old wife from Lochs.

In an example of Hebridean meritocracy and social mobility,

within fifty years Donald Stewart had become manager of the celebrated Kenneth Mackenzie tweed mill, a member of Stornoway Town Council, provost of the burgh, a magistrate, a member of the Pier and Harbour Commission and of the Stornoway Trust, and latterly and finally, the Member of Parliament for the Western Isles.

Those positions constituted a remarkable half-century for a remarkable man. In view of his other achievements, it was perhaps inevitable that Donald Stewart would stand for election to Parliament, and that he would stand in the islands. His only obstacles were his chosen political party, and his opponent.

By the late 1960s, Malcolm K. Macmillan had been the Western Isles' MP for over thirty years. It would be suggested that his appeal was waning, but his results did not suggest as much. In the two elections of 1964 and 1966, Macmillan was returned with the biggest vote, the largest percentage of the vote and the most overwhelming majorities of his political career.

In 1970, Donald Stewart would stand in the Western Isles for the Scottish National Party. The SNP had not given Macmillan or the Labour Party much trouble before. A twentieth-century creation, they had not yet contested every Scottish constituency in every election.

In eight previous elections Malcolm K. Macmillan had been challenged by just two Nationalist candidates: the party's founding leader and former Stornoway solicitor, county councillor for Benbecula, and Provost of Inverness, Alexander McEwen in 1935; and the folklorist, Gaelic activist and brother of the Raasay poet Sorley, Calum Maclean in 1951. They both finished third in fields of three runners. Moreover, the Scottish National Party had not before 1970 won a single seat at a General Election anywhere in Scotland. Its only breakthrough had been in the Central Belt seat of Hamilton at a by-election in 1967.

Having busied himself in the House of Commons in 1969 and early 1970 defending the Sabbath day against Sunday trading, protesting against excessive freight charges to the islands and sponsoring a bill to give more support to the annual National Mod, Malcolm Macmillan approached the 1970 General Election with confidence, defending a vote from four years earlier of 8,565, which in that small constituency represented 61 per cent of the total and gave him a majority of 5,733.

The result announced in Stornoway Town Hall when the last ballot boxes from the smaller southern islands had been received and counted, was nothing short of seismic. With a swing of approaching 25 per cent, Donald Stewart unseated Malcolm K. Macmillan. Stewart registered 6,568 votes to Macmillan's 5,842. Four years later the matter was sealed at another General Election. In 1974 the Western Isles Labour Party deselected Malcolm Macmillan. The former MP refused to go quietly – he was, after all, only 60 years old – and stood as the sole representative of the 'United Labour Party' against a new Labour candidate. They failed to attract 4,000 votes between the two of them. Donald Stewart was returned with a conclusive 10,000 votes. His eighteen-year term of parliamentary office was underway.

The Stornoway Trust would never rejoice in or look to exploit such a triumph, and of course Donald Stewart resigned all of his local positions upon his election to the House of Commons, but it was quietly and satisfactorily noted, regardless of political persuasions, that half a century after its inauguration, a member of the Trust had become its Member of Parliament.

It was therefore significant that the new MP's earliest interventions in the Commons reflected the concerns of the Stornoway Trust itself. In the 1920s those concerns had focused on land. In the 1970s they were focused on jobs.

The population of Lewis had fallen yet again, from 23,731 in 1951 to 21,934 in 1961, and 20,329 in 1971. Once again, it was not so steep a decline as to cause panic, and once again, Lewis maintained its position as the best populated as well as geographically largest of the Hebrides. But the search for a stimulant, or a package of stimulants, which could transform a slow fall into a steady ascent continued.

In May 1971 Donald Stewart opened a debate in the House of Commons on the specific subject of unemployment in the Western Isles.

'This is not a problem which has arisen only since the last election [of a Conservative government],' he stressed. 'As the Under-Secretary will appreciate, I say that not to absolve the Government of their responsibilities in any way but to point out that this problem is one of long duration. It has existed at least throughout my lifetime. It has been chronic and endemic for a long time.

'In the last year, the average figure for unemployment [in the Western Isles] was 25 per cent. There has been a slight improvement lately, but honourable Members will realise the serious situation that would exist in Britain if that level of unemployment were spread throughout every constituency in the country.

'Even that shocking statistic does not reveal the true position. There are about 1,000 weavers in the Harris tweed industry who are not classed as employed persons. I shall approach the Government later with a view to rectifying the cruel travesty by which these weavers are classed as self-employed persons.

'The full immensity of the problem is also masked by emigration. For lack of opportunity, the Hebridean must leave the island of his birth in search of work. Permanent "clearances" are operating in the Western Isles every year. Since the turn of the century every census has shown a fall in the population of each island. For some reason, in one of the islands there was a slight increase in 1951, but that was the only increase in population in any of the islands of the Western Isles at any census since 1901.

'The Highlands and Islands Development Board, in its 1969 report, said that another 400 had left in that year, and I believe that, when the figures are available, the coming census will show that the trend of a falling population continues.

'The passion for education in the Western Isles also acts against us. From the islands we send to the universities more students per head of the population than any other part of Britain. This testimony to the intelligence of the people means that they must perforce work other than in the land of their birth. Once they obtain qualifications, they must, because of the lack of opportunity, place their skills other than in their homeland.

'The building trade in Scotland is in a serious condition. Nearly a fifth of the unemployment is accounted for by the building trade. In the Western Isles we find no exception to this rule. In Stornoway the situation is extremely serious. It is made worse by the fact that when builders in the Isles are out of work, they leave the Isles to look for work and very seldom can be induced to return. It is difficult enough to encourage industry to come to the Western Isles, but local enterprise has also been throttled by lunatic restrictions.

'For instance, I know of a new venture in Harris, an island which has been extremely hard hit. A new textile company was set up. Looms were purchased in Yorkshire. Because the company has been brought into existence locally, it must pay for the transportation of these looms from the town in Yorkshire where they were purchased. Had it been a case of a company coming from Yorkshire, the freight charges would have been borne by the grants available.

'We are bedevilled by a transport system with abnormally high freight charges. It is essential that this barrier to development and a reasonable cost of living should be given high priority by the Scottish Office, with a view to removing or reducing substantially the burden on us.'

The Highlands and Islands Development Board, or HIDB, a specific agency with a wide-ranging and well-financed remit to lift the economy of the entire region, had opened in Inverness six years earlier, in 1965. An unimpressed Donald Stewart said: 'The effect of the Highlands and Islands Development Board has been minimal in the Western Isles. I have told the present chairman that, in the first few years of the Board's existence, it appears to me to have had a mainly mainland orientation, and I am not alone in that view. Apart from the Outer Islands Fishery Scheme, which the Board took over after it was instituted by the previous Conservative Government, we see little sign of the Board's operation in the Western Isles.

'Although we have not benefited under the Board to the extent that other parts of the Highlands have, every penny has been welcome. But the Board's expenditure must be kept in perspective. It has been pointed out recently that its total expenditure in the Highlands in the first five years was equal to the cost of eight miles of motorway. When the Scottish Trades Union Congress was demanding the setting up of such a board, it talked in terms of an expenditure of £250 million, spread over ten years, it is true. That is the kind of financial backing that the Board should have had when it was set up.

'I have said in the House before that no Government, whatever their colour, have made a real effort to grapple with the problem of unemployment in the Western Isles. But I am waiting for a sign of the will and desire to tackle the problem.

'I make the following suggestions. The first one concerns a programme of public works. The honourable Gentleman may think that this is an easy answer, but public works are essential, and many of them are long overdue in the Western Isles. We suffer many disabilities from the lack of works which should have been carried out not years but generations ago in some cases. I suggest, for instance, that the road from Rodel to Stornoway, instead of being done in instalments, should be done at once as one unit. It is necessary to transport goods from the ferry landing at Rodel to Stornoway. There is also an urgent need for a new main road in North and South Uist.

'To assist the building trade, much urgently needed building should go ahead now. I have in mind schools, for example.

'Then there are water schemes. I understand from the county councils of Inverness-shire and Ross-shire that there are schemes in the offing. I hope that the Scottish Office will look at them with favour.

'More finance should be given to the HIDB, and its powers should be increased. If it proves impossible to get the development to come north on the scale that we require, the solution is to allow the Board to initiate schemes of its own.

'Another possibility is the return of the Stranraer–Larne ferry to the Scottish Transport Group. This ferry, operating on the west coast, was kept out of the Group. It earned £700,000 in 1968. That profit should go into the pool for the benefit of the whole west coast. Instead of giving this profitable section of west-coast sea transport away to British Railways and leaving the other islands under the nationalised system, many of them running at a loss, the whole should be one. This might result in a more reasonable level of freight charges.

'Then the Government might consider the abolition or reduction of income tax for a stated period. This may seem a romantic notion. This device has been tried elsewhere with good effect. The Government should set their mind to looking at the possibilities. In any case, we pay the same tax as the rest of the country for many services which we do not enjoy.

'I want to record my support for the five-point plan put forward recently by Sir John Toothill. The honourable Gentleman will be aware of the details. Sir John said, "Why not, for a change, try stimulation instead of restriction?" I echo this for the Western Isles. Most areas in Scotland are needful, some more than others, but my constituency, on the facts, is the neediest of all. I call on the Government to do their duty.'

The fortunes of his party in the wider world waxed and waned, but domestically Donald Stewart had a relatively untroubled two decades as Western Isles MP. After his wipe-out of the opposition in 1974 he was seriously contested only once. It was by another accomplished and influential member of the Stornoway Trust, Alexander 'Sandy' Matheson. It came in 1979. Sandy Matheson reduced Donald Stewart's vote by 10 per cent and re-established the Labour Party as contenders in the Western Isles, but could not make a decisive impact on the sitting MP's large majority.

It is certain that Matheson did not expect to win, and probable that he did not want to win. He told the *Stornoway Gazette* four decades later: 'To my domestic critics I made clear that I was not standing against our old colleague and indeed friend

Donald Stewart, but for the Labour Party to which I had been sympathetic since my student days.

'In retrospect, it was a blessing. If elected, I would have been a minor backbencher in opposition with too much time on my hands away from Irene and the children. When things settled down, my response was really one of relief – I had a wife, four young children, a business to run and an awful lot to do locally.'

Those local responsibilities were always substantial. Sandy Matheson was born in Stornoway in 1942. He grew up in a generation younger than Donald Stewart but in the same ethos of civic duty. His father was the busy general practitioner Dr Alex Matheson, who also served on the Town Council.

He was partly raised by his mother's guardian, his eminent grand-uncle, the provost, councillor and founding member of the Stornoway Trust, Roderick Smith. After training at Aberdeen University to take over Roddy Smith's chemist's shop on Point Street, Sandy Matheson returned to Stornoway and was elected to the Town Council in 1967 at the age of 25. The council instantly delegated him to be one of its five *ex officio* members of the Stornoway Trust, and there began a period of service to the Trust which continued for forty years, half of its life, until he retired in 2007. For ten of those years, between 1971 and 1981, Sandy Matheson was chair of the Trust.

While chair of the Trust, Matheson was also appointed to the new Western Isles Health Board. His own career, as well as that of his father and grand-uncle, would lead him inevitably in the direction of public health. He would later reflect on the impact of the National Health Service on Lewis. In 2021 Sandy Matheson wrote:

In the period before the NHS, 1946, 1947, I was too young to appreciate the extent of what was going on, but I remember as a child the patient debate surrounding the implementation of Bevan's Act. There was a great deal of patient debate as to whether a National Health Service was the correct way of tackling the problem of providing free and quality health services to the people. Many attitudes were shaped by the people's experience in the war.

I would have thought my father, Dr Alexander Matheson, and his colleagues would have welcomed the imminent NHS, but I don't think the doctors were convinced there was compatibility of non-payment of medical bills for medical treatment and a good quality service.

Some people were afraid that the NHS would lead to a diminution of the service. Without the health service many patients would not have sought medical treatment. The whole question of having to pay meant that the patient was responding not to necessity, but ability to pay. The National Health Service was one of the fantastic things that our various governments have ever done – in creating this thing called 'the National Health service – Free for All'.

Lewis didn't get its first proper hospital until 1896 when the Lewis Hospital was created and built on Goathill Road – a mere 300 yards from where I was born. From the next 50 years it drew its income entirely from fundraising and Carnivals every year in order to pay for the hospital and treatment. The hospital was an interesting place in the early days, in that the patients were looked after by their own doctor rather than staff doctors.

During the war the Lewis Hospital took in a lot of servicemen. The patients then would have been paid for by the military. The hospital had increased turnover and better funding. Apart from the Lewis Hospital there was a County Hospital, it had its genesis in the 1920s. It was built primarily to deal with returned servicemen who had been injured, but it soon developed into an isolation hospital for the treatment of tuberculosis, which was the scourge of the island. I was aware from a very young age of the problems of TB. My own contemporaries went out to the 'sani'. Before the intervention of drugs the treatment included better diet, and sunshine. As a boy I passed the 'sani' frequently and in reasonable weather the patients slept out on the balcony rather than inside – that was because the fresh air was good for them (a flawed theory, as it wasn't until 1948/9 that streptomycin was introduced to treat TB). Incidentally if the NHS hadn't been introduced, people would not have been able to afford streptomycin.

My father ran a practice of 4,000 patients. He had regular surgeries between 9–10am, 2–3pm and 6–8pm. In those days, a lot of people didn't have telephones, so it was just as easy to go to the doctor's house as to go to the phone box. Frequently of an evening, someone would knock at the door for help, and I could go for days on end not seeing my father because he and the District Nurse were attending a 'maty' (a maternity case). 90% of the births in those days were home births – and the doctor and midwife would have to be back and fore to supervise all stages of the birth. I remember the sense of relief when he would appear home again. It always appeared to be around lunchtime that himself and the midwife would appear and have a huge lunch to celebrate the end of the process of having to look after the mother and baby.

My father, every Christmas-time, was given presents from his patients – payment in kind for the services he had provided. The bobban socks that I had were knitted by some lady in the country!

I can remember in the wee school in Matheson Road, when I had started school in 1947, we were playing in the playground and the teacher stopped me, and said: 'You're a doctor's son, there's a young girl here who has fallen and scraped her knees, will you take her in and wash her knees for her?' I wasn't even sure what a knee was at that age! It was quite an experience to find I was expected to do a job like that.

When I was a young boy, if you had a bad tooth it was taken out, a filling was not a common thing. The dentist that I had was DJ Macdonald. He was a wonderful fellow, and I would go to his surgery on Church Street, where the Police Station is now. He would talk to me about his experiences in Gallipoli. He didn't have any fancy electric drills, we would have to sit in the chair while he ground away at your filling – the whole experience of a filling was more painful than extraction. Middle-aged people used to get all of their teeth out and get false ones.

In 1947 sweets were still rationed and I remember being taken by the hand by my mother down town round the sweetie shops buying sweets and fruit. I thought we were going to have a party. My mother gathered everything up and made her way to the pier.

My mother was a quiet lady, and she went down the steps on the side of the pier and a gentleman came over and she handed over the whole bag of goodies. I remember thinking 'what a waste' and she told me they were for refugees – people escaping Russia and they found their way to Stornoway.

One of my delights as a child was going with my father on his rounds. After morning surgery, he would go to visit his home patients and I would sometimes go with him – often on school days, for a minor illness or even feigned illness precluded school but not necessarily to do something useful or active. He would go into the house and I would normally sit in the car – though sometimes I too would be allowed to go into the patient's home where I always received a warm and hospitable welcome. That's how I got to know what was going on in the country districts of Stornoway. Going out in the car with my father was a different kind of classroom for me.

I wasn't there, but I remember on one occasion my father went to visit an old lady who was bed-ridden. My father was extrovert and had a wonderful bedside manner. He was taking the lady's pulse as the lady lay there in bed and on the bedside table, he spied the Free Presbyterian monthly magazine. He looked at her and he said, 'I see you're a Free Presbyterian.' The women went into raptures afterwards and said, 'What a wonderful doctor he is – he knew by taking my pulse that I was a Free Presbyterian!'

Part of my father's work was as a social worker as well as a clinician! I remember people in great distress asking him to intervene in other matters. I remember one Saturday afternoon our whole household being disrupted because a hysterical woman came to the house because she had over-bought on her hire purchase system and the bailiffs were knocking at her door. So the doctor was there not just for her health – but to get the bailiffs off her back!

After 1948, there were still three divisions: public health was run by the local authority, general medical services were run by the Executive Council and the hospital was run by the local regional board – our hospital was managed and run from Inverness.

In 1973 all of that changed and we had the creation of Western Isles Health Board. From that time on the hospital services, general medical, dental and pharmaceutical services were run by the new Board. I was appointed in 1973 under that system. People in the Western Isles were allowed to run their own health services. One significant change since then has been the move away from medicine to health prevention and health promotion, with intervention at a much earlier stage. People were also made more aware of the need for a good diet.

In my own experience of illness, I would like to remark on how the health service has changed for the better. The steps that have been taken are absolutely remarkable in such a small area as ours. Who would ever have dreamt that cancer would become a treatable condition. That's tremendously important and people sometimes take the health service for granted, in terms of the services that are given. Without the catalyst of the NHS, I don't know where we would be.

Sandy Matheson was also the youngest provost of the burgh of Stornoway, until he helped to abolish that post in 1975. If the Stornoway Trust member Donald Stewart spearheaded a sea-change in Hebridean parliamentary representation, his colleague Sandy Matheson did the same for local government.

The Royal Commission on Local Government in Scotland, which was chaired by Lord John Wheatley, between 1966 and 1969 took a long hard look at the country's maze of councils, corporations and burghs, and recommended that the system should be picked up and shaken to within an inch of its life – which duly occurred in the consequent legislation for local government reorganisation in 1975.

The Wheatley Commission was confronted from Galloway to Shetland by 'more than four hundred local authorities: 33 county councils (4 of which were paired as "joint county councils" for most purposes), 4 county of city corporations, 197 town councils (administering 21 large burghs and 176 small burghs) and 196 district councils. These structures had mainly been introduced in the late 19th century, and were largely based on units that dated back to the Middle Ages. There was also no clear division of functions between counties, burghs and districts.'

Nowhere was that dysfunction more obvious than in the Western Isles. In recognition of their intensely Gaelic shared identity, the populated islands between Lewis and Vatersay had been part of the same parliamentary constituency since 1918. In the 1960s, however, they were still divided between two county councils. The two different island polities of Lewis and Harris were separated by a range of hills, and by the fact that one answered to Ross & Cromarty Council in Dingwall and the other to Inverness. A county boundary therefore ran from east to west between Loch Resort and Loch Seaforth, crossing the modern road on the Lewis side of the mountain known as the Clisham. Local government within Lewis was in its turn further sub-divided between Stornoway Town Council and the Lewis District Committee.

Wheatley himself proposed in 1969 that the western and northern islands, which were broadly divisible into the Outer and Inner Hebrides, Orkney and Shetland, should become semi-autonomous districts of a new overarching Highland authority based in Inverness. In the Inner Hebridean island of Skye, which was paired with its mainland seaboard of Lochalsh, that is exactly what happened. There convened a Skye and Lochalsh District Council to collect the bins in Portree, while regional councillors were sent to debate bigger matters in Inverness. Wheatley recommended that subsidiary district councils should also be maintained or established in the Highland satellites of Shetland, Orkney, Lewis, Harris, North Uist, Benbecula, South Uist and Barra.

It was not an acceptable solution for many in Orkney and Shetland, and as those island groups worked towards being given their own independent unitary authorities headquartered in Lerwick and Kirkwall, many in the Western Isles decided to negotiate for the same type of council, to be headquartered in Stornoway. They included the youngest-ever provost of Stornoway, Sandy Matheson.

In 2021, Matheson told the *Stornoway Gazette*: 'Stornoway Town Council and all the other authorities within the Western Isles opposed [the Wheatley proposals], and eventually an amendment was accepted to create a single authority. I became bound up in laying the ground for the new authority through a Joint Advisory Committee, which I chaired.'

Matheson and his Lewis colleagues found valuable allies among the councillors from the southern islands of Uist and

Barra, who were at least as interested in escaping the mainland lairds who still dominated Inverness County Council like so many monarchs of the glen, as in exploring the full potential of the Western Isles to govern themselves.

The Western Isles Islands Council, which was also known as Comhairle nan Eilean, and after the Local Government (Gaelic Names) (Scotland) Act of 1997 as Comhairle nan Eilean Siar, was born in 1975. Its boundaries were the same as the parliamentary constituency of Donald Murray, Malcolm K. Macmillan and Donald Stewart: the 100-mile-long island chain from the Butt of Lewis to Barra Head.

'The early aims and achievements of Comhairle nan Eilean were pretty impressive – the new secondary school at Linaclete; improved inter-island transport; establishment of a Gaelic policy and for my part a new and vigorous attitude towards economic development,' Sandy Matheson would recall. 'There was also the challenge of attracting new staff resident in the islands whereas local government had not previously been a career prospect.'

Comhairle nan Eilean inherited almost all of the powers and duties of the old Stornoway Town Council, apart from its synergetic relationship with the landowner, the Stornoway Trust. Since 1924 half of the ten Trustees had been town councillors, who were appointed to the Trust by their colleagues on the council. That arrangement had not only reflected the origins of the Trust as a child of the Town Council. It also ensured overlapping responsibilities between the two democratic bodies, and sharing of the local political talent pool.

It was agreed that such a disposition would be unsuitable for an all-purpose authority which represented not only all of Lewis, but also the whole of the Outer Hebrides. After 1975 the ten Stornoway estate Trustees would all be directly elected to serve four-year terms, with staggered elections for half of the membership taking place every two years to ensure continuity.

The close ties between the Town Council and the Trust had been inevitable, as one was the child of the other. There were occasional suspicions of an overly cosy relationship between the landowner and the local authority, and doubts about the amount of power invested in both. But that power had not been abused, and the crossover had also served the people of the district by offering a consistent degree of common purpose between its two elected administrative bodies.

Certain social reforms, reflective of the times, were introduced by the council directly to the Trust. For its first forty years there were no female provosts or female Trustees and no female chairs. In 1965 that all changed at a stroke when the formidable Ann Urquhart became the provost of Stornoway and therefore simultaneously the chair of the Stornoway Trust.

She had been born in Keose in Lochs in 1901, the second-youngest of thirteen children of Angus and Addie Smith. 'I hope that in my doing so,' said Ann Urquhart as she accepted the provost's chain of office, 'I may blaze the trail for women in this Burgh to come forward into public life and in due course take the chair as I am doing so now.'

Early in the 1970s, the Highlands and Islands Development Board approached the Stornoway Trust, which Sandy Matheson by then chaired, to ask about the possibility of developing a manufacturing site on some of its coastal land.

9

The Yukon Comes to Lewis

'The Arnish development came about because of the involvement of the Highlands and Islands Development Board, which was headed at that time by Sir Andrew Gilchrist,' recalled the Trust chair of the time, Sandy Matheson, of the genesis of what was later described as 'the biggest thing ever to hit Lewis'.

> I well remember Sir Andrew coming across to Stornoway and inviting myself and D.M. Smith, the factor of the Stornoway Trust, to go with him in a little boat over to the Arnish Peninsula, and explaining to us there that they had an interest in land in Lewis, and they wondered if it could be placed here. That was the beginning, and when we indicated that, yes, we were willing to talk to anyone, he put us in touch with Fred Olsen executives . . .
>
> These were challenging and educative days for me, but again I had D.M. Smith to keep us on the right track. Despite the many ups and downs at Arnish over nearly fifty years, it is still there and has – as we recognised from day one – the biggest roll-mill for tubes in Europe.

In 1974, the tweed industry was in one of its cyclical periods of decline, the economy of Lewis was flatlining and Sandy Matheson was in his third year as chair of the Stornoway Trust. Matheson's eye was always on the economic development of the island. With the visit to Lewis of Sir Andrew Gilchrist, Matheson saw an opportunity to hitch its fortunes to the colossal wealth which was about to be minted from North Sea oil. Sandy Matheson and D.M. Smith were offered a chance to divert some of the oil bonanza from Aberdeen and Lerwick down to the needy north-western islands. They seized the day.

Fred Olsen is a multinational Norwegian family company which established itself in shipping in the middle of the nineteenth century. Early in the twentieth century it expanded and diversified under the eponymous Fred Olsen, a son of the founder. By the 1970s, with yet another Fred Olsen at the helm, Olsen was engaged in shipbuilding, aviation and, most crucially and inevitably, in the burgeoning North Sea oil industry.

Arnish Point is a small, bare peninsula which juts out into Stornoway Bay, helping to shelter the harbour. On its northern, protected side is a deep-water anchorage known as Glumaig. It is within the estate of the Stornoway Trust. Andrew Gilchrist's intention was to introduce Fred Olsen, who had made known their interest in Scottish oil-industry construction, to Arnish and to its proprietors, the Trust.

It was a prospect of Leverhulme dimensions. In their initial planning application early in 1974 Olsen detailed their requirement of '200 acres of Stornoway Trust land at Glumaig Bay, Arnish, for a supply and fabrication base . . . the company say that they could be employing 1000 men'. The plant at Arnish Point alone would involve a £6 million investment.

In the 1970s, 1,000 new construction jobs in Glasgow or Aberdeen would have been welcomed. In Lewis at any time, they would both change the face of the island and guarantee its immediate economic well-being. The Stornoway Trust would have denied its own founding principles if it had looked such a gift horse in the mouth.

The Town Council, which had not yet been replaced by Comhairle nan Eilean as the planning authority, was not unreservedly committed. Councillors were concerned that the island's energy supplies and its transport and communications infrastructure might not be configured to serve a large industrial town, and they asked for a meeting of all public bodies 'to identify the strain likely to be caused by the development and to ensure proper Government financing of the infrastructure'.

Town councillors were also fully aware of the concerns of the churches about Sunday work. In fact, in that or any other matter, the churches could hardly have imagined a more sympathetic landowner than the Stornoway Trust. The Trustees were all native or adopted Leòdhasaich. Most of them were adherents of either the Free Church or the Free Presbyterian Church of Scotland. Some of them were elders of those congregations, and even if they belonged to neither, they had been raised by families which were at the very least respectful of the Lord's Day, in communities which paused almost all financial and social activities for twenty-four hours after midnight on every Saturday of the year. Stornoway Trustees were, in short, more likely than not to be practising Sabbatarians themselves. The Trustees were also all elected to either the Trust itself or to the Town Council. They were fully aware that any insult to the Sabbath would not be unnoticed by their churchgoing constituents and would be paid for at the very next elections.

Sandy Matheson and D.M. Smith had naturally anticipated the Sabbath question. 'The one real issue was over Sunday work,' said Matheson much later, 'and negotiations on this were very complicated especially as Olsen had said they would withdraw if any details of the entire plan were released prior to agreement in principle.' They had nonetheless obtained from Olsen a guarantee that 'only essential maintenance work will be carried out on Sundays'.

Other doubts were comparatively negligible. Some of Lewis's other employers, such as the tweed mills, were concerned that a thriving construction yard in the vicinity would lead to unreasonable wage demands or loss of workers from their own shop floors. They were right. There was no answer other than to pay comparable rates. Some Gaelic activists and campaigners from outside the region voiced quiet worries about the dilution of a Gaelic-speaking fishing and crofting culture. That was a difficult anxiety to fly past a board which was composed almost entirely of native Gaelic speakers, who were prepared to counter that without young people there was no future for Gaelic in Lewis, and without decent employment prospects there would be no young people.

The huge construction yard, docking facilities, offices and aircraft-hangar-sized fabrication and assembly halls rose out of the moor and sea at the south side of Stornoway harbour in 1974. A subsidiary company named Lewis Offshore Ltd was responsible for the development, but it was then and thereafter referred to in Lewis simply as Arnish.

It was the fiftieth anniversary year of the Stornoway Trust. Those who noticed such things could remark that the development signalled the Trust coming of age. It was hosting, with sensitivity to local interests, a project which would offer to Leòdhasaich the kind of work and rewards that had previously only been available overseas. Graduates from another of the Trust's devolved responsibilities, Lews Castle technical college, had only to walk down the road to sell their skills. The college itself teamed up with management at Arnish to provide youngsters with special courses, freshly adapted to the needs of late-twentieth-century deep-sea oil extraction. Not a single croft needed to be resumed.

So the island of Lewis was introduced to the industrial world through the buccaneering oil industry of the 1970s and 1980s, rather than through paternalistic monopoly capitalism in the 1920s.

Leòdhasaich were not unfamiliar with the rest of humanity. Their men had circumnavigated the Earth. Their people had settled and worked in North and South America, in Asia and Australasia, in London and Glasgow. By the 1970s, they received in Stornoway daily newspapers by aeroplane, and most of them were connected to television networks. They knew about trade unions, cowboy employers and winters of discontent. They knew, in short, what they were signing on for at Arnish – quick and plentiful money in exchange for long, hard hours in an unscrupulous trade. There was little room for sentiment, and in the event none was exchanged.

The voices of former Arnish workers were recorded by MacTV for a 2022 BBC Alba documentary titled *Arnish*. Their consensus is that few people regretted the experience, and a great many saw the benefits: 'At the end of the week you had a big wage packet and earned much more than you would as a builder . . . I bought a brand-new car at the age of 21 . . .'; 'People left offshore work [in the North Sea itself] to work at the yard because the pay was better'; and 'Joiners were paid £40 a week at that time. My first Arnish wage was £140 . . . it was like winning the lottery for a young man.'

If the Stornoway Trust and the Lewis workforce were surprised by anything, it was the stop–go, boom-and-bust nature of North Sea oil contracts. Throughout the 1970s the yard's orders, and therefore its hundreds of workers, seemed relatively secure. They first built a steel barge the size of a narrow football pitch called *Lonka*. At 94 metres long and 27 metres wide, 6 metres deep, with a draft of almost 5 metres, the mighty *Lonka* was unlike any vessel previously manufactured anywhere in the Hebrides. She was completed and launched in Glumaig Bay in April 1977. After *Lonka*, there came a short, broken string of orders for a rig conversion and various rig jacket contracts. The latter required large tubular steel members and therefore utilised Arnish's possession of a rare industrial mill – 'the biggest roll-mill for tubes in Europe' – which was capable of rolling 6-inch-thick steel.

Throughout those heady first years, on Friday and Saturday nights the town of Stornoway came to resemble what different people described as the Wild West during a gold rush. Pubs thrived and clubs opened. A small commercial base was suddenly flushed by the injection of a very large amount of disposable cash. 'The butcher said that instead of buying a pound of mince people were buying four steaks, they were buying prime cuts ... everyone bought new VCRs and TVs and cars.' Smith's Shoe Shop on Cromwell Street did unprecedented trade in vast quantities of industrial footwear, or 'Arnish boots'.

'Arnish changed the whole island, because people were making a bit of money, and they could build houses, which they did, especially young people, some built big houses.'

As well as 1970s consumer goods, Arnish workers embraced 1970s industrial culture. The yard was at first unionised and in the inflationary national economy of the time there were both wildcat and official strikes, largely around the matter of wages. Health and safety measures were, compared to later years, negligible. When the deadlines for delivery approached, Lewis Offshore management brought in sub-contractors from elsewhere in Scotland and the United Kingdom. Both friendships and enmities between locals and 'subbies' ensued, at work and at leisure, with the fights being far more visible than the amities. With the landladies and landlords of Stornoway parish at bursting point, a ship was hired to anchor in Glumaig Bay and accommodate the visiting temporary workers.

The 1981 census told its own story. It recorded the population of the island of Lewis as 21,546. That was not only an increase of 6 per cent on the population ten years earlier of 20,329, but also the first time since before the First World War that the Lewis population had risen.

There was no doubt about the driving force. Insofar as any other Hebridean islands were comparable to Lewis, in the 1970s or at any other time, they fared nowhere near so well. Skye also benefited from the oil boom through a construction yard at Kishorn in south-west Ross, but its population rose only fractionally from 7,183 in 1971 to 7,276 in 1981, an increase of 1 per cent. The fifth-biggest British island of Mull had no new industry in its immediate vicinity and rose in the same period by just 173 people, from 2,024 to 2,197. Only in the northern Shetland islands, which were actually processing and exporting offshore oil, as well as building ancillary constructions, was there a better demographic improvement than in Lewis.

Skye and Mull still had a dwindling base of crofting and fishing, without the tweed weaving which survived there only in Portnalong. They would both, in the following decades, benefit from massively increased tourist industries which, assisted financially by the successors to the Highlands and Islands Development Board, and structurally by a road bridge to the mainland, in the twenty-first century threatened to overwhelm Skye during the visitor seasons.

There had long been a small, niche tourist industry in Lewis, which the Stornoway Trust had encouraged and exploited through its provision of the modestly profitable fishing and shooting parties. These had, at the very least, put Lews Castle into profitable employment during the 1930s. The attractions of Lewis to modern visitors in search of scenery and antiquity were not so obvious as the Cuillins of Skye but were nonetheless substantial. Even if a tourism culture was wanted, however, and in the case of Lewis it was not, the bigger island seemed to demand some major focal manufacturing for export industry whose profits would first of all kickstart its insular economy, and then pour down into households, retail outlets and other smaller enterprises. The 1970s proved that such a model worked in Lewis, for as long as it could be sustained.

That period of energetic activity reflected back on its originator, the Stornoway Trust itself. The November 1977 elections attracted fifteen candidates, a record number, for five Trustee positions. There was a public hustings in the town hall the night before the poll was held for the first time since the war. 'Ever since the Trust began negotiations a few years ago with Lewis Offshore Ltd for the lease of land at Arnish for a fabrication base,' commented a journalist, 'interest in the work of the Trust has increased.' The turnout rose from its usual 10–15 per cent to 23 per cent of 4,500 voters. It would slip back again but continued to illustrate an essential truth: when the landowner needed to be called to account, an established procedure existed to do just that. In the words of the Trustee Kenny MacIver, 'There are, of course, complaints. But if there is real discontent then people can do something about it. They are both owners and tenants. And as landlords, the Stornoway Trust has been necessarily very responsive to local needs and opinions.'

Oil may have been the only industry which could create and then support an investment the size of the Arnish construction yard in Lewis. But oil was quickly revealed to be the opposite of sustainable, in every sense of the term.

The strikes that marked the yard in the late 1970s were reflective of industrial relations in the rest of the United Kingdom. They were not always unreasonable and they were usually popular with the workforce. In June 1976, just before the launch of the *Lonka*, 140 platers and welders walked out to press their demand for an island allowance, among other standard benefits. In common with other contractors, Fred Olsen were paying island allowances to imported mainland workers, to ease their transition to the Outer Hebrides. Olsen did not expect to pay island allowances to native island workers. Nor did they anticipate a Lewis workforce so quick to realise its own worth and its bargaining power. It was suggested that Olsen were partly attracted to the Hebrides by the prospect of training up a docile, biddable body of employees who would be only too happy to escape the oppressive daily grind of the soil and the sea and would cause no trouble to their benevolent paymasters. If that was ever true, if Fred Olsen harboured such delusions for a moment, it betrayed a profound ignorance of recent Lewis history and it would soon be exploded by events.

That sense of their own agency among Leòdhasaich workers was to a degree attributable to the bargain struck by the Stornoway Trust. Fred Olsen had been obliged by the Trust not only to limit Sunday work and commit to an apprenticeship and youth training programme, but also to recruit their employees as far as possible from among locals. The Trust was naturally pragmatic about the implementation of its demands. When Olsen announced that they needed to bring in 400 skilled workers, such as pipe fitters and pressure pipe welders, to complete a conversion contract, the Trust did not demur. The local Lewis workforce was nonetheless made fully aware of its unusual value.

In April 1979, 600 men elected to strike over canteen food. 'The food for those on the rig,' reported the *Press and Journal*, 'is taken in hot plates from the canteen. Yesterday, however, there were about eighty meals short and when the men went ashore to the canteen there was no food left there. The men, who had been complaining about the food for some time, decided to go on strike.'

In November of the same year there was a critical stoppage over 'safety measures ashore and afloat, [following an] incident last Monday when a man fell overboard from the ferry which takes the workers on the crossing between the yard and the Drillmaster rig, which is being converted into a production platform for the BP Buchan Field'.

> Last week the men proposed that a working party was formed to carry out certain improved safety measures which the company had agreed to before the workforce returned, but this was rejected by the management, who said that the site was not unsafe in any way.
>
> Although the men decided on Saturday to return to work today [Monday], incoming workers wanted the company to pay their lodging allowances for the time they had been on unofficial strike. The management informed the men that if they sign on for work this morning, they would pay their weekend lodging allowances. A company spokesman emphasised that the site was perfectly safe and that any work carried out would only make the site safer. The proposed improvements

could easily be carded out after the full workforce returned . . .

In the event the men did not immediately go back. A further site meeting took 800 of them out when the Lewis workforce joined the 'subbies' in solidarity with their claim for accommodation expenses. The entire workforce was then sent letters of dismissal. Lewis Offshore's project manager at Arnish, Stewart Hunter, met with members of the Stornoway Trust to inform them of the seriousness of the situation. There were three orders at the yard, including one from the new council, Comhairle nan Eilean, for the four-car, thirty-five-passenger, eighteen-metre ferry for the South Uist–Eriskay route, *Eilean na h'Oige*, and the Drillmaster rig conversion which was, Hunter told the Trustees, in danger of being towed away for completion elsewhere. The Highland organiser of the Amalgamated Union of Engineering Workers (AUEW), Ian Macfarlane, who frowned on and spoke publicly against unofficial strike action, finally persuaded both sets of workers that it was in everyone's best interests for them to return.

But when Olsen eventually pulled out in 1982, it was with little ceremony. 'We came back from holiday,' remembered a Lewis man, 'went into work, and were handed a letter straight from the copying machine saying, thanks for your effort, we're closing down.'

Within the year another operator was found. Olsen was replaced at Arnish by an enterprise which had been born twenty years earlier out of the post-war Venezuelan oil boom.

A Dutch company, Heerema Engineering Services, entered the infant North Sea oil industry in the early 1960s as the offspring of Constructora Heerema, which had been established in 1948 to construct and install drilling platforms in the rich oil fields of Lake Maracaibo in Venezuela. One of Heerema's first conditions on taking over the Arnish yard was to deunionise Lewis Offshore Ltd. Considering that the AUEW had been a voice of moderation and constructive sense among warring factions in Lewis for the previous eight years, that was both unfair and self-defeating.

The heady, hardworking early years of Arnish ended with the departure of Fred Olsen and led to a period of boom and bust. 'For the first few years the work was steady,' said one Lewis worker, 'then after a few years we were paid off. Then they'd get a new contract and you'd go back maybe for a year ... I often thought, there must be something better I could do ...'

Looking back in 1989, the experienced Highland journalist Bill McAllister would write in the *Press and Journal*, 'The Dutch firm Heerema took over Arnish from Olsen in 1982, but were hit badly four years later when Shell abruptly cancelled a £2 million subsea template order which was already half built. But by October 1986, a £6 million BP Cleeton contract led Arnish to claim it was now the only yard in the country with a full order book for the next eighteen months. Almost exactly a year ago, the Lewis yard went on a "care and maintenance" basis and, last Christmas, Heerema finally pulled the plug. The isles' flirtation with North Sea oil was over.'

Like Olsen before them, Heerema left without sentiment. 'I remember being asked,' said Sandy Matheson, who in 1988 was still chair of the Stornoway Trust, 'along with my friend and colleague [the Trust factor] D.M. Smith, to go to Amsterdam, and we thought, oh good, something is going to come of this. So at no little expense and no little stressful travel we made our way to Amsterdam. We were ushered into an office and sat down, and with no tea or hospitality, all they said was, we have asked you to come here to tell you that we are closing the yard. They could have done that in so many other different and helpful ways. And that was it.'

The divorce from oil was not immediate or absolute. Until the very end of the twentieth century, and in some quarters beyond the millennium, there was optimistic talk of new oil fields being opened not only west of Shetland, but also west of Lewis, which would clearly put Arnish in a prime marketing position.

The succession of Atlantic oil from North Sea oil was not a fantasy. Nor was it ever likely to be a painless transition. There was undoubtedly oil under the bed of the North Atlantic Ocean. But it was a deeper and wilder stretch of water than the North Sea. Throughout the 1990s industry experts predicted that 'deep water reserves will have an enormous impact on the domestic market ... the huge economic potential on offer might surpass the North Sea investment and returns far beyond the turn of the century'. The realisation of that potential would depend on constructors realising that 'interest in concrete platforms is increasing, as the sea depths west of Shetland make steel jackets to sit on the seabed impractical. Concrete platforms are more stable, and while the capital cost of building may be high, they offer easier maintenance with lower running costs.'

Such possibilities were alive in 1990, when the Stornoway Trust transferred the lease of the yard at Arnish to a team of former managers which included several Leòdhasaich. Colin MacIver, Murdo MacIver and Norman Macaskill had all worked at Arnish since the 1970s. Peter Webster first worked at the yard in the early 1980s, as did finance director Henk Graauwmans and David Walker.

Four years later, they were still in position and the yard was ticking over. At the very beginning of 1994 Peter Webster of the management team told Angus MacDonald of the *Press and Journal*, 'If I could have one wish, it would be continuity of work in this yard.'

'At present,' reported MacDonald, in what was almost an elegy to the old yard and a nervous welcome to the new,

> It can keep an average workforce of two hundred, as well as up to a hundred office staff, employed until the end of the year. This is a substantial boost for the economy of Lewis, where the bedrock sectors of tweed-making and fishing are struggling.
>
> But it is only a breathing space for the yard, which has deliberately aimed at a low but constant level of work. It is competing hard for more, generally smaller, contracts. But if the proverbial 'big one' is thrown its way, it could, Webster claims, easily handle it – even if it means further investment to add to what he claims are already excellent facilities.
>
> The yard opened as the oil construction industry climbed into its boom years: one of several such yards throughout the Highlands. Built on Arnish Point at the entrance to Stornoway Harbour, it reached its own zenith as the seventies ended. A rig conversion for BP and numerous jacket contracts dominated the view from the centre of Stornoway . . .
>
> The main port in the Western Isles resembled the Yukon with a mixture of people walking the streets, the likes of which had not been seen since the height of the herring fishing about half a century before.
>
> Now budgets are tighter and, as oil companies push costs down, forcing yards to bid for work at lower prices, the Arnish facility has developed an expertise

for small contracts employing around 100 workers, which the larger yards with higher overheads would not take up.

'You are only as good as your last job,' according to Webster. 'Potential clients will speak to people who have just had work completed by you, or to people with work in the yard. You have to keep bidding, contacting people in the industry, and ensuring the jobs are done on time to the required standard and within budget.'

With the hundreds working in the yard in the early eighties came huge spending power – but it did not last. Fred Olsen, the Scandinavian shipping magnate who built the yard on land leased from the Stornoway Trust, began pulling up the stakes – initiating a period of uncertainty – before selling it to Dutch company Heerema in 1982.

Then came the management buyout. 'It was a well-informed gamble,' said Peter Webster. 'I knew it was a good facility and a good workforce with a good reputation. The fabrication shop can handle everything from sub-sea templates to jackets, decks, piles, and topside modules. There is a deep-water load-out facility, and a mill that will roll six-inch-thick steel plates. We have added to that and the workforce is highly skilled and loyal.'

The management team inherited a deunionised yard from Heerema. Following negotiations with the local representatives of the General, Municipal, Boilermakers and Allied Trades Union, or GMB, an overtime ban was closely followed by recognition of the GMB and the re-unionisation of the workforce of 100 people. 'It is in the best interests of all parties that the union should be recognised,' said Henk Graauwmans, hoping that a renewed union agreement would 'prevent any wildcat action while giving the workforce experienced officials on whom to call as this year's pay negotiations get under way'.

'The facilities sell themselves,' said Webster, 'but getting people to come here to see them is the main hurdle. People think we are on the edge of the world, but it makes little difference whether you are shipping finished steelwork from Stornoway or Spain.

'One guy phoned and asked how many days it would take, getting here from London. I told him to take the early shuttle to Glasgow the next morning and he could be home that evening after a whole day's work.

'Another guy just about melted in his first half-hour in my office. He was wearing several jumpers because he thought the temperatures would be sub-zero.'

Lewis Offshore was 'the Highland oil fabrication industry's guerrilla', concluded Angus MacDonald, 'picking off the smaller contracts and sub-contracts for larger work . . . There is also a possibility that, in the longer term, following another large oil find by BP west of Shetland, oil will be discovered in significant quantities around the Western Isles.

'Lewis Offshore has already set out its stall at some of the most prestigious exhibitions in the industry, as a fabricator and a supplier of support services to companies which might be interested in exploring and exploiting the Atlantic. That would shift the periphery into the centre, with Lewis Offshore, and the Western Isles, in a prime position.'

The periphery of Lewis would be shifted to the centre of Scottish politics not by undersea oil, but by surface wind.

10

Blowing in the Wind

In June 2003 the United Kingdom's energy minister welcomed the news that the Arnish yard in Lewis, which had been mothballed, would shortly reopen, 'to undertake its first order for wind energy' for its new operators, Cambrian Engineering.

Cambrian had been contracted to build turbine towers for an offshore wind farm in the sea east of East Anglia, and they announced that the work would be done at Arnish.

'This is a fabulous result for the Isle of Lewis and the whole renewables industry,' said energy minister Brian Wilson. 'It sends out the strongest possible message that renewable energy is not just about environmental benefits but also offers huge manufacturing potential ... Arnish has been brought back from the dead by the renewables revolution and I believe that we can have many more excellent results of a similar nature as the process develops.'

Brian Wilson knew his subject matter. His family home was on the west side of Lewis. His relationship with the Stornoway Trust went back more than thirty years to his days as a Highland newspaper editor and journalist, and his interest in wind power was almost as longstanding.

There were two main motivations for the Trust's excursion

into large-scale wind farming in Lewis. One was to 'get a thousand people back into Arnish'. The other was to generate so much electricity – 'one percent of Stornoway Trust land could provide one percent of Scotland's energy' – that the UK government would be obliged to lay a large new interconnector cable between the Hebrides and the north-western mainland.

That would in its turn enable a virtuous circle of further island renewables initiatives, which could then offer further work to a Lewis workforce based chiefly at Arnish. The consequences for the island economy had already been clarified in the 1970s. Hundreds of people had earned good money at Arnish Point, resulting in increased trade for shops, garages, pubs and restaurants. Houses had been built and expanded. Butchers had sold fillet steak rather than mince. Within Stornoway and the Trust's own estate, that caused very little controversy. The crofters of Point and Back were generally as approving of job creation at Arnish – and of annual royalties dispersed by wind-farming companies – as were most of the people of the town.

Elsewhere it could be a different matter. If people did not particularly benefit from a booming Stornoway they were disinclined to be enthused by the phenomenon. There was also among some professional Leòdhasaich a lingering attachment to Celtic twilight; a druidical desire to invest Lewis stone and Lewis heather with semi-sacred properties that should not be sullied by ranks of large wind turbines. And there were those who feared that the two established economic pillars of weaving tweed and catching fish would be pulled down by the Arnish yard luring younger workers away from the trawlers and the Hattersley looms.

Cambrian Engineering had bought the yard in 2000, out of the receivership into which it had fallen after the collapse of the management buyout. A thirty-year-old fabrication company, Cambrian had turned to wind in the late 1990s, having seen which way it was blowing.

Climate change, and the impact of fossil fuels on the planet's environment and atmosphere, had been a simmering issue for decades. Action to combat the damage done by greenhouse gas emissions was only taken when a big majority of the international scientific community convinced a plurality of governments that the matter was urgent and getting worse.

The large-scale development of renewable energy sources had also been explored, not least in the Highlands of Scotland, throughout the twentieth century. Massive hydroelectric schemes were built in several mainland glens to introduce domestic electricity to the region. Serious attempts to harness the power of the sea tides and the constant wind of the north and west of Scotland had been made since the 1960s.

North Sea oil and gas may have seemed plentiful, but they were limited resources. By definition they were non-renewable. As their stocks were exhausted, by the end of the twentieth century even power companies looked around for other means of turning profits. Their eyes fell naturally on forms of energy which neither deep-fried human life nor would run out within thirty years.

So interest from all quarters – political, financial, scientific and popular – in wind and hydro power were building as the reputation and the remaining stocks of fossil fuels fell. Their lines of fortune and favour crossed, one going down and the other up, early in the twenty-first century.

Following the adoption and ratification of the United Nations' Kyoto Protocol to combat climate change in 1997 and 2005, the United Kingdom was among the first of 192 signatory countries to legislate against fossil fuels. In 2008 its

Parliament passed a Climate Change Act which committed the UK government to reducing emissions of the six major greenhouse gases by 80 per cent before 2050.

Whatever its impact on the atmosphere, the 2008 Act and its successors had a profound potential and actual effect on the nature of the UK economy in general and the Scottish economy in particular. Phasing out oil, gas and coal from industrial and domestic energy supplies opened the door wide to renewable, 'clean' resources. Insofar as those resources were wind and water, an almost permanently breezy and wet archipelago on the north-western fringe of Europe should have been poised to cash in – nowhere more than the windiest, wettest islands on the archipelago's own Atlantic edge. The phrase 'the Saudi Arabia of renewable energy' was coined first for Lewis and the other western islands, and only later applied optimistically by politicians to the rest of Scotland. The fact that Lewis had not only wind, but also a construction yard capable of producing wind turbines by the score, gave the island what looked like an unapproachable lead in the new energy game.

The Stornoway Trust soon involved itself. The Trust not only had the yard and the workers in its estate, it also had many square miles of uninhabited, uncultivated upland moor, across which the wind blew unproductively on most days of the year. The oil industry was clearly not about to offer a secure and dependable future to workers at Arnish. The 2001 census had shown the island's population slipping back again, to 18,489, which was a disturbing decline of 14 per cent from the Arnish high point of twenty years earlier.

Early in the twenty-first century the Stornoway Trust as landowner, along with Comhairle nan Eilean Siar as planners, interested two large companies in the potential of wind power production on Lewis.

The companies were Amec Foster Wheeler, usually abbreviated to Amec, a multinational consultancy, engineering and project management company headquartered in London, and British Energy, which was at the time the United Kingdom's largest electricity generation company, operating eight formerly state-owned nuclear power stations and one coal-fired power station.

Between them those parties founded Lewis Wind Power, a subsidiary company dedicated to taking forward a vision of Lewis as an economy thriving on the production, servicing and export of electricity generated by renewable energy.

By 2004 Lewis Wind Power had already formulated its proposals. Given the size of the main industrial players, and the ambition of all involved, they were unlikely to be modest. In the event, Lewis Wind Power proposed to build in northern Lewis the largest wind farm in Europe. It would contain 234 turbines, each one 122 metres high. Once developed and in operation the Lewis wind cluster would supply 10 per cent of Scotland's electricity and 6 per cent of the UK's immediate renewable targets. Three hundred jobs would be instantly created, and when it was up and running the wind farm on Barvas Moor was anticipated to earn £2.1 million a year for the Stornoway Trust as landowners, and the same amount to be shared among crofters whose grazings hosted turbines. It was once again a proposal whose grandeur and industrial ambition matched those of Lord Leverhulme a century earlier. For not dissimilar reasons, it also would not be fully realised.

British, Scottish and Hebridean politics had all changed radically since the establishment of the construction yard at Arnish thirty years earlier. In 1987 the Stornoway Trustee Donald Stewart's seventeen-year tenure as Member of Parliament for the Western Isles came to an end. He retired undefeated, and the seat promptly reverted to the Labour Party.

Calum MacDonald had been born and bred within the estate of the Stornoway Trust. He was a 31-year-old Rubhach, an alumnus of Bayble School, the Nicolson Institute and Edinburgh University who had spent three years in his 20s as a teaching fellow at the University of California in Los Angeles before returning home to help with the family business. Without Donald Stewart, the SNP vote almost halved, and MacDonald comfortably took the Western Isles seat.

Ten years later he became a member of a Labour government which devolved most domestic legislation to a freshly elected assembly in Edinburgh. Calum MacDonald was Under-Secretary of State at the Scottish Office which delivered that assembly, and in doing so effectively legislated itself out of power.

In the first elections for the new Scottish Parliament, which were held in 1999 under a system of proportional representation, the Labour Party won the Western Isles constituency vote. Another 30-year-old Gaelic-speaking man, a native of North Uist named Alasdair Morrison, won a five-cornered race with just over half of the vote. Morrison, who had previously been a broadcast journalist, was appointed in the first Scottish Assembly as Deputy Minister for the Highlands and Islands, and Gaelic and Deputy Minister for Enterprise and Lifelong Learning.

When Calum MacDonald had won four back-to-back elections and Alasdair Morrison had won two, along came the Lewis wind farm.

The extent and ambition of Lewis Wind Power's plans were such that the company wanted to build parts of its wind ranch on land to the west and north of the Stornoway estate. In the early 2000s, that meant striking deals with some of the other landholders, such as Galson and Barvas estates, which were then still in private hands. The people of the Stornoway Trust had a clearly defined method of expressing their approval or disapproval of estate policy, on wind turbines or anything else, through the ballot box and through elected, accountable Trustees. The people of Galson and Barvas, who comprised the remainder of northern Lewis, had no such means of democratic censure.

The pressure group Mòinteach gun Mhuileann, or Moorland Without Turbines, MWT, was formed in the west side township of Bragar on the Barvas estate. From the very beginning it ran an openly political campaign, and enjoyed remarkable success.

In a leaflet titled 'The Case Against Turning Lewis Into a Wind Power Station', which the people who would become Mòinteach gun Mhuileann distributed around the west of the island in 2004, they introduced themselves as 'a group of Westside residents, all of us born and brought up here. We are not normally campaigners, but prefer a quiet life. However, the scale and industrial nature of the massive windfarm development proposed for North Lewis, and the fact that we love our local moorland and the whole of our native island, has galvanised us into action.'

Having identified themselves as straightforward country folk, they then lined up the manifold branches of the enemy:

1. Amec and British Energy (partners in a new company, Lewis Windpower). 'Amec is a multinational construction company that, despite producing a sustainability report and policies, continues to be involved in a series of controversial and destructive

projects that threaten its reputation. The company is subject to campaigns at local, national and international levels, because of its activities in the UK, North America, South America and Africa.' (Taken from Friends of the Earth, Amec Counter Report, 2002. British Energy's vision statement taken from their own website is 'to be the world's leading nuclear energy company'.)

2. Politicians. The government is attempting to meet its Kyoto energy saving targets, and appears to see wind power stations as a major way of achieving that aim.

Brian Wilson MP, who, according to John Price of Amec, first invited the company to Lewis to look at the Arnish yard. Mr Wilson has had many contacts with Amec over the years, in his previous position as Minister for Industry, Energy and Construction, and in his present job as the UK special representative on trade and reconstruction in Iraq. Mr Wilson is also the founder of the West Highland Free Press.

Calum MacDonald MP and Alasdair Morrison MSP have made clear that they are fully behind the proposals to turn huge areas of the Lewis moorland, close to villages, into industrial windfarms run by outside companies.

Convenor Alex Macdonald, Vice Convenor Angus Campbell, and other councillors (especially Labour councillors) on Comhairle nan Eilean Siar. Up until the recent public meeting on the Amec proposal in Bragar, our council representatives had managed to keep very quiet about what is potentially the biggest change to the environment of Lewis since the peatlands were formed. 'Surely it is the role of our councillors, MP and MSP, whom we elected, to represent the views of the community and not their own views.' (Quote from Charlie Stewart, Bragar meeting, 13th April)

3. The landlords. Stornoway Trust, Barvas Estate and Galson Estate have already signed legally binding Heads of Agreement with Amec/British Energy. Although the turbines will be on village common grazings and peat cutting areas, shareholders were not asked for their consent.

That coalition of multinational industrialists, local and national politicians and estate owners was, according to Mòinteach gun Mhuileann, planning 'the industrialisation of our landscape . . .'

This will be Europe's largest windfarm. It will stretch from Ness in the north, follow the moor side of the road all the way down to Barvas, then take over both sides of the road across the Barvas moor. Just before Newmarket it will curve off between that village and the Barvas hills, and south to the Pentland road. If you turn off at Barvas, the same windfarm will be before you all the way to Bragar.

Numbers vary for the Amec/British Energy proposal from 240 to 300 turbines . . . The turbines will be about 135m high, to the top of the blade. We understand a 100m diameter circle will be resumed at the base of each turbine. The developers state the roads will be 5m wide, but once drainage, borrow-pits, and peat banking are included, the affected area may be up to 16m wide. Approximately 140 km of road will be needed for the Amec scheme alone . . . Overhead cabling, probably in the form of pylons, will be required to connect the sites to the planned interconnector at Arnish. The power will then be carried down to electricity markets in Southern Scotland and England.

Once planning applications are granted, it is relatively easy to add and extend after that . . . Amec and British Energy are here because they expect to make massive amounts of money out of their massive turbines – Amec themselves have stated some £96m per annum.

Although we don't know the final figures, Calum MacDonald MP states that £6m per annum will be paid to the community. John Price of AMEC has put the figure at £3–6m. This money will be split four ways (not equally). The landlords and crofters will get an amount per megawatt, to be shared 50/50. This seems good for the landlords, especially those who do not stay within the development location, and so will not have to live with it on a daily basis. We believe the crofters' 50 per cent will go to Grazings Committees. If it is then shared out, any money individual crofters get (probably less than £2000 per annum) would, of course, be taxable. An amount per MW will also go to community councils in the affected areas, with the fourth share going to a Western Isles wide fund set up by Comhairle nan Eilean Siar.

Different answers have been given as to how many jobs these large-scale windfarms will provide. We believe that more jobs could be created if communities owned and ran their own small renewable energy schemes (as is being investigated in North Harris). The profits from these community schemes could then be ploughed back into the local economy to create jobs and prosperity. Jobs at the Arnish yard are not guaranteed, and if the jobs do come, how long will they last?

Tourism is worth about £40m a year to the Western Isles. VisitScotland have published a 190-page report, Investigation into the Potential Impact of Wind Turbines on Tourism in Scotland. Four out of five of the visitors interviewed said they came to Scotland for the beautiful scenery and almost all said they valued the chance to see unspoilt nature. More than half agreed that wind-power sites spoiled the look of the countryside, saying that one of their main attractions is the fact that they are few and far between. Over a quarter said they would avoid parts of the countryside with wind developments.

The £3–6m or so being left in the Western Isles by the Amec development may be substantially less than revenue lost from tourism, and will not go to the many businesses that will be adversely affected.

The visual intrusion will be so enormous it is hard to imagine. It will be almost impossible not to see turbines in Lewis. The constant movement will involuntarily draw the eye to them. Even at night we might have no escape from them . . .

Unusually large numbers of some of our scarcer breeding birds are found on the moor. Together with the rare plants and mammals found there, it makes the moor a very important place. The construction of a large-scale windfarm would mean the permanent loss of plants and other wildlife – there's also the risk of disturbance and collision – which combined could have a devastating effect on the area's wildlife. (Taken from RSPB leaflet 'Lewis and windfarms'.)

Councillors and Calum MacDonald MP have stated that they want these large-scale wind developments in order to 'arrest and reverse the downward spiral of depopulation'. However, it remains unclear how hosting the world's largest windfarm for a multinational company will do this. The amount of money the Council will get from it will not make a major difference to their budgets, and short-term construction jobs will have no long term impact on our economy.

MWT was anxious to stress that it was not opposed to wind farms, only to wind ranches:

> We are not against wind power, but we are against the large scale developments being proposed at present . . . Let's look at options which will benefit us more, and blight us less.
>
> '. . . a community-owned windfarm of just two turbines would produce more revenue for the local community than the £350,000 per annum that the developer (on Eisgean Estate) is promising from 125 turbines.' (From article on windfarms by Calum MacDonald MP, on www.calummacdonald.co.uk.)
>
> Information from our MP from West Highland Free Press (30.4.04) – 'a 250 MW community-owned Western Isles windfarm would bring the Comhairle £30m per annum . . .'

We believe that, if local communities want them, small numbers of turbines could be sensitively placed – well away from people's homes and with regard to wildlife – and that such developments could be of great benefit . . . And contrary to the Council's stance, there is evidence that the island's housing market is more buoyant than it has ever been. Houses in rural Lewis, even those in poor condition, sell readily and at good prices. At least one school in North Lewis has increased its roll, due to families coming into the area.

How much longer will buyers queue up to purchase houses when they know the island will be blighted by massive windfarms? And how long will it be before families begin moving out, going elsewhere to find the peace and beautiful environment which drew (or kept) them here in the first place?

What was more, and which within a few years would be the conclusive tactical weapon in a drawn-out battle of words, the unassuming mass of Barvas Moor was actually an environment of global significance. '"The blanket bog of the Lewis moor is acknowledged as equivalent to the African Serengeti or Brazil's tropical rainforest,"' asserted MWT. '"The moor therefore carries European designations of Special Protection Area and Special Area of Conservation, and is also recognised under the UN Ramsar Convention." (Taken from RSPB leaflet, 'Lewis and windfarms'.)'

That extended account formed the bulk of the anti-wind farm case in Lewis in the 2000s. The Stornoway Trust, in collaboration with national and local Labour Party politicians, was supposedly inviting ruthless multinational companies to make fortunes from the Lewis peat bog, paying only pennies in compensation for destroying the wildlife, landscape and the local tourist industry, all for the benefit of people in 'the south'. It succeeded over the following months and years in dominating the Lewis wind-farm narrative.

The first ominous signal came at the 2005 General Election, before the matter was resolved. Calum MacDonald entered his fifth campaign with a majority of 1,074 from a turnout of 13,159.

His Scottish National Party opponent Angus Brendan MacNeil, a personable 34-year-old Gaelic teacher from Barra, did not openly campaign against wind farms. As MacNeil's own party was committed to an expansion of renewable energy throughout Scotland, that would have been difficult.

But an appetite for change shared by just a few hundred voters had always made an impact on the fortunes of the smallest parliamentary constituency in the United Kingdom, as the Western Isles, or Na h-Eileanan an Iar, was still. Its size, which was perennially, uniquely guaranteed by the Boundary Commission on the grounds of geographical remoteness and cultural significance, meant that Na h-Eileanan an Iar was almost always a marginal seat, where even a small swing could tip the balance. It was an eccentric marginal, with a loyal attachment to sitting representatives, but a marginal nonetheless.

There was a small swing of 4.5 per cent against the Labour Party throughout Scotland in May 2005, which lost them two seats to the SNP. In Na h-Eileanan an Iar, the swing was 10 per cent, which meant that Calum MacDonald's constituency was one of the two which fell to the SNP. Angus MacNeil was returned as the islands' second nationalist Member of Parliament, with a majority of 1,441 votes from a slightly increased turnout.

Two months after the General Election, in July 2005, the members of Comhairle nan Eilean Siar, the Western Isles Council, met to debate giving planning permission to Lewis Wind Power's proposal.

The eventual application was for 234 turbines, each one 122 metres high. The councillors asked for 'the removal of 25 sensitive turbines proposed close to houses or in areas of archaeological interest'. It would still be 'the world's largest wind farm'.

An estimated 300 jobs, they heard, 'would be created during construction, while the community-owned Stornoway Trust Estate would receive £2.1 million a year for the landowners and the same again for the crofters'.

The proposal, the council heard, had attracted 4,191 objections, 'mostly from within the islands'. Planning officer Alasdair Banks nonetheless recommended approval. Stornoway councillor Keith Dodson welcomed it as 'an opportunity to breathe life and prosperity into the islands'.

Dodson's colleague Anne MacDonald pointed out that the population of rural Lochs, which she represented, had fallen by two-thirds in the century between 1901 and 2001. 'The government has given our area a title of "outstanding natural beauty",' said Councillor MacDonald. 'It is beautiful, but beauty does not put food on the table. Renewable energy can be a vital part of our economy and it is the only sector that offers the prospect of a substantial number of jobs.'

Councillors voted to approve the development. It had one further obstacle to overcome. The final decision would be taken by the devolved Scottish government at Holyrood in Edinburgh.

Since its inception in 1999 the executive of that 129-seat assembly had been a majority coalition between Labour and the Liberal Democrats. Member of the Scottish Parliament Alasdair Morrison of the Western Isles had been an active participant in the governing coalition. At the third Holyrood elections in May 2007, both the national and the Hebridean representation changed dramatically.

Nationally, the total Labour vote declined only slightly, by just over 1 per cent. But the Scottish National Party collected large numbers of additional votes from some minority parties which had favoured independence, leapfrogging it marginally ahead of the Labour Party in both numbers of seats and numbers of votes. The SNP still had too few of either to form a majority, and so they entered into a grace-and-favour coalition arrangement with the Scottish Conservative Party. Seventy-two years after Malcolm K. Macmillan had beaten its founder Alexander MacEwen in the Western Isles, and 37 years since the Stornoway Trustee Donald Stewart had become its first MP to be returned at a General Election, the SNP took office as a ruling party in a Scottish parliament. Their new responsibilities included a final word on planning consent.

In the Western Isles constituency in May 2007 a straight switch of a few hundred voters saw the SNP's candidate Alasdair Allan overthrow Alasdair Morrison. Allan, a 36-year-old from the Scottish Borders who had worked for the SNP in various backstage positions since leaving university, became the second Member of the Scottish Parliament for Na h-Eileanan an Iar.

The switch of coalition administrations at Holyrood from Labour–Liberal Democrat to Scottish National Party–Conservative meant that following the May election of 2007 the latter suddenly had the final word on such big planning matters as the Lewis wind farm.

The new government announced its decision a year later.

In April 2008 the new energy minister, the MSP for Argyll and Bute, Jim Mather, said that the scheme, which had been further reduced to 181 turbines, would 'devastate a globally significant peatland . . . and would have had significant adverse impacts on rare and endangered birds living on the peatlands, in breach of European habitats legislation'.

On top of that, the Scottish Government said, 'nearly 11,000 islanders had objected to the scheme, which had been supported by the Western Isles council and the island's main community trust'.

The energy minister said that 'the decision did not mean his Scottish National party administration in Edinburgh was opposed to wind farms in the Western Isles or in general'. Ministers were 'pushing ahead with plans for a new sustainable "green" energy programme for the islands, which experts believe has amongst the greatest renewable energy potential of any part of the UK'.

'Nor does today's decision alter in any way this government's unwavering commitment to harness Scotland's vast array of potentially cheap, renewable energy sources,' he added.

Lewis Wind Power was 'bitterly disappointed' by the decision. The farm would have brought 400 jobs to Lewis, injected £6 million a year in rental payments and other benefits to the island, said the frustrated developer, and meant a crucial 'interconnector' to take electricity to the mainland would have been built.

'Sadly all of this has been lost because of the government decision which, we believe, represents a huge missed opportunity,' the firm said.

A Lewis crofter sympathetic to the Moorland Without Turbines pressure group said, 'I'm absolutely delighted, and I'm delighted for the people of Lewis who fought long and hard against this, on the same grounds as the wind farm has been rejected. The environment, the landscape and the peatlands are worth far more than any wind farm.'

He said that many crofters fully supported his criticisms. 'You can't replace peat with concrete, and ever hope to get away with it. There are thousands and thousands of years of vegetation growing and rotting, year after year after year. That's how it was intended to be. But I would fully support going offshore as long as it doesn't have any marine conservation consequences.'

At the next election to the Scottish Parliament in 2011, Alasdair Allan increased his majority by 30 per cent.

The future of Lewis as the Saudi Arabia of renewable energy, with the Stornoway Trust at its hub, was put on hold. It was not abandoned. The double-barrelled benefits of renewable energy dividends, coupled with the good jobs offered by turbine construction at Arnish, were impossible to ignore. While the campaign of Mòinteach gun Mhuileann adversely affected the fortunes of the local Labour Party, it made little impression on the Stornoway Trust. At the following elections, Trustees in favour of wind-power developments were returned to office. The Trust's east-coast and urban constituents were either in favour of wind farms, or they were as profoundly uninterested in the subject as the west-coast members of Mòinteach gun Mhuileann were absorbed.

In the short term, for obvious reasons, any progress would have to be made without the support of the island's Member of Parliament, Member of the Scottish Parliament, or the Scottish Government in Edinburgh. Throughout the first two decades of the twenty-first century, the government of the United Kingdom, presented with such inexplicable dilemmas in the Outer Hebrides, seized the opportunity to postpone laying an expensive interconnector from the western littoral to Lewis across the floor of the Minch. A longer and more costly cable was instead offered like a rebuke between the northern Scottish mainland and the wind turbines of the cooperative archipelago of Shetland.

As other, smaller wind turbines and clusters slowly emerged from the Lewis heather, some of them run by community groups and some of them on Stornoway Trust land, the Stornoway Trustees, councillors and Lewis Wind Power persevered with their grander plans.

In 2012, 2015 and finally successfully in 2021, and following exhibitions and public consultations in Stornoway Town Hall in 2018 and 2019, Lewis Wind Power proposed a new wind farm on Stornoway Trust land alone, to the west of Stornoway. It would contain 'up to 24 turbines with a tip height of up to 180m and 9 turbines with a tip height of up to 156m, a total of up to 33 wind turbines'.

The farm was estimated to offer 'community benefit payments' of £900,000 a year, paid into an independent trust to distribute to local projects and organisations. There would also be annual rental payments to crofters whose grazings were affected, and to the Stornoway Trust as landlords, of as much as £1.3 million.

'Stornoway Wind Farm,' said Lewis Wind Power early in 2022, 'is the largest of the three consented wind farm projects with a grid connection in place and is therefore key to the needs case for a new grid connection with the mainland. Indeed, the UK energy regulator Ofgem has stated that it will support the delivery of a new 450 MW cable if the Stornoway and Uisenis projects are successful in this year's Contract for Difference allocation round.'

This time it was approved. With even the Royal Society

for the Protection of Birds persuaded to withdraw its routine objections, Scottish ministers joined Comhairle nan Eilean Siar in supporting the initiative. 'I would like to thank the Stornoway Trust for their support in the development of this project over the last twenty years,' said the company's Claire Jones with discernible relief, 'and the Comhairle nan Eilean Siar for their constructive approach to the planning aspects of this development.'

Later in the year Ofcom finally agreed to build its interconnector cable across the Minch, linking renewable energy production in the Western Isles to the United Kingdom's national grid and allowing island generators to export clean electricity. 'We are delighted to see confirmation from Ofgem that the interconnector will go ahead to link the Western Isles to the mainland,' said project manager Logan Black. 'A lot of work has been done locally to get to this stage and we will continue our work to build Stornoway wind farm as soon as possible. The interconnector, and in turn Stornoway wind farm, will bring huge benefits to the local community, Scotland's net zero ambitions and the UK's energy security.'

In February 1994 estate bailiffs of the Stornoway Trust noticed a net running out into Glumaig Bay from Arnish Point. The bailiffs called the police and swooped upon the yard's couple of hundred staff. Following interviews, two night-shift workers were detained. Managing director Peter Webster declared himself 'shocked' and warned the rest of the workforce of the consequences attendant upon poaching fish.

Lewismen did not need to be warned of the dangers of being caught poaching. The incident suggested partly that Arnish had joined the fabric of everyday life in Lewis, partly that Arnish workers were testing the mettle of the owners of public land in defending their fishing rights, and partly that there was a good run along that part of Glumaig Bay, which had probably yielded decent hauls throughout the twenty-year lifetime of the yard.

With and without turbine production, the construction yard at Arnish continued its roller-coaster career. Following a troubled spell as an outlier of the Fife contractor Burntisland Fabrications, the yard entered the 2020s as the property of the Belfast shipbuilding giants Harland and Wolff – a company which had coincidentally been for many years until 2019 a subsidiary of the Arnish founders, Fred Olsen Ltd.

Orders arrived and work sporadically recommenced. Arnish, in tandem with its old BiFab sister yard at Methil in Fife, would in future, said Harland and Wolff, be devoted to the construction of jackets and turbines and other essentials for a booming Scottish renewable energy sector.

Between 2001 and 2011, the population of the island of Lewis rose by 6 per cent, from 18,489 to 19,658.

11

A Quiet Revolution in the Western Isles

In November 1992 a display advertisement appeared in the Situations Vacant columns of newspapers and magazines across Scotland. It announced a vacancy for the £25,000 per annum position of estate factor at the Stornoway Trust. D.M. Smith was retiring.

The successful candidate would be joining 'a unique organisation, which serves a community on the Isle of Lewis'.

> It exists to manage a publicly owned estate of land, including the town of Stornoway and the former Parish of Stornoway. The Trust's activities are fundamental to the quality of life on the island and its continuing success directly benefits the local community.
>
> The Estate Factor is the essential link between the local community and the actions of the Stornoway Trust. Responsible to ten publicly elected Trustees, the position commands considerable local prestige and respect. Apart from managing all Trust employees, the Factor directs Trust activities on a daily basis ... We are seeking a diplomatic and interpersonally

skilled individual who is sensitive to the needs of the local community. An experienced administrator and staff manager, you will be familiar with the demands of estate management and will have had some exposure to Crofting Law. A knowledge of Gaelic/Island culture would be viewed favourably.

The advert's proud and correct assertion that in 1992 the Stornoway Trust was a 'unique' organisation, confident in its organic relationship with the quality of life in Lewis, conveying prestige upon its office holder, and respectful of Gaelic culture, made it as much a mission statement as an advertisement. It left unstated the fact that the holder of the position was capable of moulding the character and purpose of the job – and consequently of the Stornoway Trust itself.

By the twenty-first century virtually every person in the public life of Stornoway and its surrounds had put in at least one shift on the Stornoway Trust. But in the whole of its first hundred years only three men had worked as estate factor.

They divided the century more or less evenly between them. Edwin Aldred served for thirty-three years between 1928 and 1961. D.M. Smith was factor for thirty-two years between 1961 and 1993. Iain MacLennan Maciver took up the post of estate factor in 1993 and enjoyed his thirtieth anniversary in 2023, the 100th year of the Trust.

Iain Maciver was a 37-year-old native Gaelic speaker from Laxay in Lochs who arrived at the Stornoway Trust from a position as community education officer with Comhairle nan Eilean and from the Scottish Crofters Union, of which he had been a founding member and chair. Twenty-four years into his role as estate factor, in 2017, Iain Maciver was elected by his fellow Hebridean crofters to represent the Western Isles on the

Crofting Commission, as the old Crofters Commission had been renamed. It is impossible to imagine another factor of any other Highland estate appearing on either body, let alone being nominated to chair one and being elected by crofters to represent Lewis on the other. Those details spoke volumes about the Stornoway Trust, as well as the qualities of its factors.

As Donald Murdo Smith would discover, the Trust factor was respected well beyond the Trust's community. A year before his retirement, Smith was made a Member of the British Empire in the 1992 New Year Honours List.

In the autumn of 1993, the Stornoway Trust celebrated its imminent seventieth birthday by proposing to double its electorate. The reform was an indirect product of the Conservative government's failed local government community charge, or poll tax. When the poll tax was repealed it was replaced by a council tax. Neither the council tax nor the short-lived poll tax required a local valuation roll, which consequently fell into disuse. As an appearance on the valuation roll had been the yardstick for franchise to Stornoway Trust elections, a legacy of the days before universal suffrage when property owners and ratepayers monopolised elections, another policy was required.

The Trust's chair in 1993, Iain MacLeod, announced that at the next elections in March 1994, everybody within the Trust's boundaries who appeared on the electoral roll would have a ballot. Henceforth, if a resident could vote for a Member of Parliament, he or she could also vote for a Stornoway estate Trustee. That would have the immediate effect of increasing the constituency from 5,000 to 10,000 voters. 'This will mean that the 10,000 people on the electoral roll in the trust area will be eligible to vote,' said Iain MacLeod. 'However, candidates for election and those who nominate and second them will all require to be owners or occupiers of property on the estate.'

The established elections involving 5,000 voters, which usually attracted low turnouts of a few hundred people, or 10 per cent to 15 per cent of the electorate, cost the trust £5,000 to mount every two years, so in an effort to keep the cost down 'trustees will serve for six years, with half retiring every three years'.

In the months after Iain Maciver took up his new job in Stornoway, the attention of the media was drawn to events at three estates on the West Highland mainland and on two small Inner Hebridean islands.

Assynt is a classically beautiful assembly of Highland hills, lochs and glens. It sits between the mountains and the sea directly across the Minch from Lewis, on the same line of latitude as Stornoway and Point. On a clear day the two estates look at each other.

By the 1990s the substantial Assynt estate had been in the hands of the Vestey family and its immensely successful conglomerates for most of the twentieth century. Edmund Vestey, the latest of his line to assume responsibility for that parcel of the Highlands, decided in 1989 to carve 21,000 acres and thirteen crofting townships, containing slightly more than 100 people, from the rest of the property, rename that tract North Lochinver estate, and sell it for £1 million to a Scandinavian property company. Three years later Scandinavian Property Services Ltd went into liquidation. The Assynt branch of the Scottish Crofters Union then agreed to form a limited company, Assynt Crofters Trust, to bid for the 21,000 acres and thirteen townships, to bring them under the control of the crofters, and to develop the area by initiating projects such as house building, job creation and tree planting.

The Assynt Crofters Trust raised hundreds of thousands of pounds from locals and from well-wishers. Each crofting family on the estate contributed at least £1,000. Caithness and Sutherland Enterprise, the local arm of the development company Highlands and Islands Enterprise, donated £50,000. Scottish Natural Heritage gave a grant of £20,000. Highland Regional Council donated £10,000. A public appeal raised over £130,000 from 824 different individuals, including political and cultural figures such as the local Member of Parliament, Robert Maclennan, Ray Michie, Alex Salmond, Winifred Ewing and Charles Kennedy, and the Gaelic rock band Runrig. A secured loan of £90,000 was received from Highland Prospect Limited, a company set up by Highland Regional Council to promote investment in the Highlands.

The first two bids of Assynt Crofters Trust for their land were rejected. The third, of £300,000, was accepted. On 1 February 1993 the people of Assynt took over their land and renamed it, for a third and last time within a few hectic months, North Assynt Estate.

Having carried, for almost all of the twentieth century, on its own broad shoulders the burden of responsibility for making the reformed ownership of Scottish land work as a practical going concern in the cruel real world, suddenly the Stornoway Trust was no longer alone.

A domino effect followed. 'It opened the dam and became the way forward for community land ownership,' said Assynt Crofters Trust director Bob Cook later. 'That wouldn't have happened if we had not done it.'

Small and neglected islands and estates with ageing, declining populations, diminishing prospects and apparently little to lose joined the long march.

The twenty crofters on the 4,500 acres of Borve and Annishadder estate in north Skye negotiated an amicable purchase with a modest price tag from their friendly local landowner in 1993.

Across the Cuillin Sound from Skye, in the small island of Eigg relations between the residents and their proprietors had been far from amicable for years. A former Olympic bobsleigh competitor named Keith Schellenberg, who thought of himself as operating a benevolent despotism on the island, bought the property on April Fool's Day in 1975, and fell out with the inhabitants in ways which led to arson attacks on his property. Schellenberg sold up after twenty years to an enigmatic German artist called Gotthilf Christian Eckhard Österle, or Maruma.

It made irresistible copy for national newspapers. 'The 43-year-old, chain-smoking, beret-wearing professor (self-styled),' reported *The Independent,* 'spouts New Age philosophies and creates paintings by burning the canvas. His name is said to have come to him as a sign, apparently written in puddles of water.

'The islanders rarely saw him. Nevertheless, they were well disposed to him, until he sold all their cows (except one, Barney). The previous owner, Keith Schellenberg, was none too popular, either. A former British bobsleigh captain, he reciprocated the feelings of his tenants, describing them as "drunken, ungrateful, lawless, barmy revolutionaries".'

It was Hebridean landownership through the eyes of a satirist. Amusing to most, infuriating to many and terrifyingly insecure to the fifty or sixty people who had to live under it. The Eigg affair as much as any other illustrated the insufferable nature of the private ownership of tracts of land upon which real people lived and worked and tried to raise families. If Eigg was fortunate enough to fall occasionally into the hands of a 'good' private landowner, such as the liberal Runciman family who had it for forty years in the middle of the twentieth century, it could not be touted as a triumph. If the people of Eigg waited for a little while, another bad one would soon appear, as duly occurred when the Runcimans sold out to the first in a succession of rogues in 1966. And nobody could vote Keith Schellenberg or Maruma out of office.

In the summer of 1997, following a fundraising campaign even more colourful and switchback than at Assynt four years earlier, but with greater certainty of success, the locally staffed and accountable Isle of Eigg Heritage Trust announced that it had bought the island on behalf of its residents. No fewer than 10,000 individual contributions had raised £1.5 million. Shortly afterwards the new Scottish Office minister Brian Wilson formed a public Community Land Unit at the headquarters of Highlands and Islands Enterprise in Inverness, with the specific brief of assisting and helping to fund any and all such initiatives. Tectonic plates were shifting beneath the edifices of Highland landlordism.

The first of the Lewis jigsaw pieces to be slotted in beside the Stornoway Trust occurred just a year after the Eigg buyout, when the 1,700 acres of Bhaltos crofting estate in the far west of the island was bought from its private owner by Bhaltos Community Trust, taking five townships and their croftlands and grazings into democratic local ownership. The declared aims of the Trust's 100 members and eight elected directors were familiar to anybody who was acquainted with the older and larger community landowner in the east of Lewis. They were:

> To acquire and manage the lands and resources comprising the crofting estate of Bhaltos, Isle of Lewis, for the benefit of the whole community of the estate.
> To promote and assist effective utilisation of the

resources of the Bhaltos crofting estate and the creation of sustainable development therein beneficial to the community thereof.

To improve the social, economic, educational and cultural environment of Bhaltos Estate community.

To conserve and improve the natural environment of Bhaltos Estate.

To preserve as far as possible all items of archaeological interest on the Bhaltos Estate and to encourage archaeological study and exploration on the estate.

Smaller islands and estates such as Knoydart on the north-western mainland and Gigha off the coast of Argyll continued to transfer from private to community hands. In the year 2000 the Scottish Land Fund was established with National Lottery capital of £10 million, rising to £15 million, 'to help communities buy their land from their landlords'. In 2003 the Scottish Parliament in Edinburgh passed a Land Reform Act which crucially gave crofting communities the statutory right to buy their estates from landowners who did not wish to sell.

Throughout the Western Isles, within hailing distance of the Stornoway Trust, the larger dominoes then began to fall. In 2003 the 55,000 acres of northern Harris, which contained more than half of the island and its people, including the town and port of Tarbert, was bought by the North Harris Trust, whose constitution allowed for governance by twelve elected local directors representing defined township areas and a representative of the conservationist John Muir Trust.

In 2006 the 3,000 people of the islands of Benbecula, South Uist and Eriskay bought the 93,000 acres of South Uist

Estates from a shooting and fishing syndicate for £4.5 million, creating the largest democratically owned domain in Scotland. The Stornoway Trust was suddenly in terms of acreages only the second-biggest community landholder in the country, although it remained the best populated. 'Our aim,' said the elected trustees of Stòras Uibhist, 'is to put the interests and wellbeing of the islands' inhabitants at the heart of all our activities. We are developing and supporting the natural, social and economic assets of the islands to foster a vibrant and sustainable economy; reverse population decline; protect local crofting practices; and generate employment opportunities for future generations.'

The year after the South Uist buyout, in 2007 the 58,000 acres of Galson estate in northern and western Lewis was bought by Urras Oighreachd Ghabhsainn, the Galson Estate Trust. It was another significant initiative. Twenty-two crofting townships with almost 2,000 people from the Butt of Lewis down to the northern border of Barvas sat on those 58,000 acres. Not to be left out, in 2016 Barvas Estate Trust was formed as a community company to purchase the 34,580 acres of Barvas estate land.

In 2010 a new umbrella body was established to represent Scottish democratic community-owned estates. The fore-and-afts and plus-fours of the old Scottish Landowners Federation were clearly unfit for that purpose. When Community Land Scotland was created, half of the land surface and three-quarters of the entire population of the Western Isles lived in a community estate.

In 2015 their numbers were further boosted by the successful culmination of the longest attempt by a local trust to buy its land from an unwilling proprietor. Pairc Trust was formed in one of the most neglected and depopulated districts of

Lewis in 2003. Only a dozen years later did those 28,000 acres with eleven townships arrive in the hands of the 400 people of South Lochs.

In another landmark initiative, in 2010 the 110 people of West Harris adopted the ownership and management of their 17,853 acres from the state, on whose behalf it had been managed by the Scottish Department of Agriculture and Fisheries since the 1930s.

Within ten years the population of West Harris had increased by 50 per cent. Early in 2020 Calum MacLeod, the policy director of Community Land Scotland, spoke at a Burns Supper in West Harris to mark that tenth anniversary.

'In 2010,' said MacLeod, 'there was no affordable housing in West Harris; one of the biggest problems facing any island community. Now four affordable house plots have been sold for private builds and there are ten properties, either already built or under construction in collaboration with Hebridean Housing Partnership.

'In 2010 there were no business units to let. Now there are eight business units and one office for lease across three sites. They're all occupied.

'There are new tourism facilities generating income for the community. Seven camper van hook-ups; five camping spots, and toilet and shower facilities.

'There's new infrastructure. Pontoons. Renewable energy generated by wind turbines and a hydro scheme. All delivering environmental benefits for the community and, ultimately, the planet.

'There's Talla Na Mara, this amazing community building we're privileged to be sitting in tonight. A fantastic asset for the community in all sorts of social, economic and cultural ways.

'There are more jobs. The Trust employs six members of

staff and the restaurant here in Talla Na Marra has created eight seasonal jobs. And there's the employment supported through the business space the Trust provides.

'All of these things have combined to make West Harris a better place in which to live and, increasingly, to work.

'Most preciously of all, there are now more people living here.

'Back in 2010 the resident population of West Harris was 119 folk. There was only one child under 5 years of age living in the community.

'Incredibly, that population has risen to 152 people in just ten years. There are now seven children under 5 and twenty-two people aged under 18 living here. And there are ambitions to increase the resident population still further by the end of this year.'

In 2015 the 1,000 residents of the 11,400-acre Carloway estate in the west of Lewis bought their ancestral land – which, containing as it did the Callanish standing stone formation, was more ancestral than most. It would be managed by the democratically elected Carloway Estate Trust. The people of the 27,000 acres of Bays of Harris in the east of that island, and the 5,000-acre tidal realm of Great Bernera, also in the west of Lewis, were in 2023 taking their own hopeful steps towards the same community ownership.

By 2017, only 547,690 acres, or less than 3 per cent of the total land area of Scotland, had been taken into community ownership. But 70 per cent of that total, almost 400,000 acres, was in the Western Isles. It was no accident that this occurred where it did, when the capital of the Outer Hebridean archipelago, in the main island of a unified parliamentary constituency and seat of local government, had been the centre of a community owned estate since 1924.

Just over 100 years after the men came back from the First World War and started raiding dairy farms, and almost exactly 100 years after Viscount Leverhulme paid tribute to the spirit of the people on a hill outside Stornoway, the age of autocratic private landlordism was dead and buried in the island of Lewis and in the rest of the Western Isles.

Appendices

Stornoway Trust Factors
(formerly known as Chamberlain of the Lews)

Captain A.M. Fletcher (Interim Chamberlain)	1924
Hugh MacLeod (Chamberlain)	1924–26
Edwin Aldred (Factor)	1926–61
D.M. Smith (Factor)	1961–93
Iain Maclennan Maciver (Factor Designate)	March 1993
(Factor)	April 1993–

Stornoway Trust Elected Chairs

Provosts/*Ex officio* Chairs

Kenneth Mackenzie	1922–25
Louis Bain	1925–30
Alexander Maclennan	1930–33
Roderick Smith	1933–39
Alexander John Mackenzie	1939–59
Donald James Stewart	1959–65
Mrs Ann Urquhart	1965–68
Donald James Stewart	1968–70
Alasdair Macdonald Matheson	1970–71
Alexander Matheson	1971–75

Chairs

Alexander Matheson	1975–81
James Macrae	1981–83
John Crichton	1983–89
Iain Archibald Macleod	1989–99
Kenneth Angus Maciver	1999–06
Charles Bruce Nicolson	2006–12
Murdo Murray	2012–15
Calum Maclean	2015–18
Norman A. Maciver	2018–

Stornoway Trust Elections

Trustees elected by voters on Ratepayer's Roll

28 February 1924
Dr John Pringle Tolmie
John Macritchie Morrison
Murdo Maclean
Norman Mackenzie
Angus Smith

17 November 1925
Dr John Pringle Tolmie
John Macritchie Morrison
Kenneth Mackenzie (Declined to accept office)
Norman Mackenzie
Angus Smith

4 December 1928
Dr John Pringle Tolmie
Colin Scott Mackenzie
Roderick Adam Morrison (Filled vacancy of K. Mackenzie 1926)

John Macritchie Morrison
Angus Smith

1 December 1931
Kenneth Macdonald
Colin Scott Mackenzie
Murdo Macleod
Ossian Macaskill
Donald John Mackenzie

4 December 1934
Kenneth Macdonald
Ossian Macaskill
William Mackenzie
George Macleod
Ebeneezer Mackenzie

7 December 1937
Ossian Macaskill
Kenneth Macdonald
Ebeneezer Mackenzie
Murdo Macleod
David Tolmie

4 December 1940
Roderick Smith
William John Tolmie
Murdo Macleod
Alexander G. Macleod
Hugh Mackay Matheson (Filled vacancy of K. Macdonald 1939)

8 December 1943
George Stewart
Roderick Smith

Alexander Macleod
Captain Thomas Carr Macdonald (Filled vacancies D. Tolmie and H. Matheson 1940)
John Macleod

3 December 1946
Angus Matheson Macdonald
Angus Macleod
John Macleod
Roderick Smith
George Stewart

6 December 1949
Abraham Langley
Angus Matheson Macdonald
John S. Maclean (Filled vacancy of Angus Macleod 1948)
Roderick Smith
George Stewart

1 December 1952
William John Macdonald
Allan Angus Macleod
John Macleod
Roderick Smith
Alexander John Maclean (Co-opted to fill vacancy 1953)

6 December 1955
Alexander John Maclean
Allan Angus Macleod
Angus Fraser Macleod
Roderick Smith
William John Macdonald (Co-opted to fill vacancy 1956)

9 December 1958
William John Macdonald
Alexander John Maclean
Roderick Smith
Angus Fraser Macleod
Donald Maclean

12 December 1961
William John Macdonald
Alexander John Maclean
Donald Maclean
Angus Fraser Macleod
Allan Angus Macleod

8 December 1964
William John Macdonald
Alexander John Maclean
Donald Maclean
Allan Angus Macleod
Angus Fraser Macleod

12 December 1967
Donald Macdonald
William John Macdonald
Alexander John Maclean
Donald Maclean
Angus Fraser Macleod

8 December 1970
John Crichton
William John Macdonald
Alexander John Maclean
Donald Maclean
Donald Mackenzie

11 December 1973
John Crichton
William John Macdonald
Donald Mackenzie
Alexander John Maclean
John Maclennan

28 October 1975
Alasdair Macrae Mackenzie
Murdo Macleod
William Macleod
James Macrae
Alexander Matheson

8 November 1977
John Crichton
Donald Macdonald
William John Macdonald
Alexander John Maclean
Donald John Macsween

6 November 1979
Reginald Frank Apps
John Maclennan
Allan Angus Macleod
James Macrae
Alexander Matheson

5 November 1981
John Crichton
Donald Macdonald
William John Macdonald
Alexander John Maclean
David George Thompson

8 November 1983
John Maclennan
Allan Angus Macleod
Iain Archibald Macleod
Donald John Macphail
Alexander Matheson

6 November 1985
Reginald Frank Apps
John Crichton
Donald Macdonald
William John Macdonald
Kenneth Angus Maciver

4 November 1987
John Maclennan
Iain Archibald Macleod
Murdo Macleod
Donald John Macphail
Alexander Matheson

7 November 1989
John Crichton (Died in office – February 1994)
Donald Macdonald (Died in office – October 1992)
Donald Hugh Morrison Maciver
Kenneth Angus Maciver
Kenneth Nicolson

5 November 1991
Neil Macdonald
Iain Archibald Macleod
Murdo Macleod
Donald John Macphail
Alexander Matheson

29 March 1994
Malcolm Macfarlane
Donald Hugh Morrison Maciver
Kenneth Angus Maciver
Angus Macleod
Charles Bruce Nicolson

25 March 1997
Neil Macdonald Graham
Neil Macdonald
Iain Archibald Macleod
Alexander Matheson
Roderick John Murray

7 March 2000
Robert John Mackenzie Frater
Donald Hugh Morrison Maciver
Kenneth Angus Maciver
Charles Bruce Nicolson

26 March 2003
Neil Macdonald Graham
Calum Maclean
Iain Archibald Macleod
Alexander Matheson
Murdo Murray

28 March 2006
Fiona C. Cowan
Robert John Mackenzie Frater
James Macarthur
Norman Angus Maciver
Charles Bruce Nicolson

APPENDICES

24 March 2009
Donald F. Crichton
Calum Maclean
Norman Macleod
Murdo Murray
Zena Stewart

27 March 2012
Jonathan Maciver
Norman A. Maciver
Cameron M. Macleay
Callum Ian Macmillan
Malcolm Macrae

26 March 2015
Donald F. Crichton
Calum Maclean
Colin Maclean (Resigned in January 2019)
Murdo Murray (Resigned in March 2017)
Alexander John Murray

27 March 2018
Murdo F. Campbell
Norrnan A. Maciver
Donald A. Macleod (Resigned in February 2020)
Catriona Murray
Donald Nicholson

Co-opted to fill vacancies April 2019–March 2021

Iain Macaulay
Charles Bruce Nicolson
Kenneth Angus Maciver

30 March 2021
Donald Finlayson Crichton
Calum Murdo Macdonald
Mairi Ishbel (Marisa) Macdonald
Calum Maclean

Former Trustees (Stornoway Town Council)

1924 (March)
Provost Kenneth Mackenzie
Bailie Hugh Macleod
Bailie Louis Bain
Councillor Ex-Provost Roderick Smith
Councillor Samuel Ranger

1924 (November)
Provost Kenneth Mackenzie
Bailie Louis Bain
Bailie Samuel Ranger
Councillor Roderick Adam Morrison
Councillor William John Tolmie

1925
Provost Louis Bain
Bailie George Stewart
Bailie Samuel Ranger
Councillor Murdo Maclean
Councillor Ex-Provost Roderick Smith

1926
Provost Louis Bain
Bailie Alexander Maclennan
Bailie George Stewart
Councillor Mrs Julia Fraser
Councillor Hugh Matheson

APPENDICES

1927
Provost Louis Bain
Bailie Alexander Maclennan
Bailie George Stewart
Councillor Donald John Mackenzie
Councillor William John Tolmie

1928
Provost Louis Bain
Bailie Alexander Maclennan
Bailie Hugh Matheson
Councillor Donald John Mackenzie
Ex-Provost Roderick Smith

1929
Provost Louis Bain
Bailie Alexander Maclennan
Bailie Hugh Matheson
Ex-Provost Roderick Smith
Councillor Donald John Mackenzie

1930
Provost Alexander Maclennan
Bailie Hugh Matheson
Bailie William John Tolmie
Ex-Provost Roderick Smith
Councillor Donald John Mackenzie

1931
Provost Alexander Maclennan
Bailie Hugh Matheson
Bailie William John Tolmie
Ex-Provost Roderick Smith
Councillor Alexander John Mackenzie

1932
Provost Alexander Maclennan
Bailie William John Tolmie
Ex-Provost Roderick Smith
Councillor Mrs Julia Fraser
Councillor Alexander John Mackenzie

1933
Provost Roderick Smith
Bailie William John Tolmie
Bailie Alexander John Mackenzie
Councillor Mrs Julia Fraser
Councillor Mrs Isabella Whitaker

1934
Provost Roderick Smith
Bailie William John Tolmie
Bailie Alexander John Mackenzie
Councillor Mrs Julia Fraser
Councillor Mrs Isabella Whitaker

1935
Provost Roderick Smith
Bailie William John Tolmie
Bailie Alexander John Mackenzie
Councillor Mrs Julia Fraser
Councillor Mrs Isabella Whitaker

1936
Provost Roderick Smith
Bailie William John Tolmie
Bailie Alexander John Mackenzie
Councillor Mrs Isabella Whitaker
Councillor Donald Gunn

1937
Provost Roderick Smith
Baillie John Kennedy
Bailie Alexander John Mackenzie
Councillor Mrs Isabella Whitaker
Councillor Donald Gunn

1938
Provost Roderick Smith
Baillie John Kennedy
Bailie Alexander John Mackenzie
Councillor Mrs Isabella Whitaker
Councillor Donald Gunn

1939
Provost Alexander John Mackenzie
Bailie Mrs Julia Fraser
Bailie John S. Maclean
Ex-Provost Roderick Smith
Councillor John Kennedy

1940
Provost Alexander John Mackenzie
Bailie Mrs Julia Fraser
Bailie John S. Maclean
Councillor Donald Gunn
Councillor Walter Lees

1941
Provost Alexander John Mackenzie
Bailie Mrs Julia Fraser
Bailie John S. Maclean
Councillor Donald Gunn
Councillor Walter Lees

1942
Provost Alexander John Mackenzie
Bailie Mrs Julia Fraser
Bailie John S. Maclean
Councillor Donald Gunn
Councillor Walter Lees

1943
Provost Alexander John Mackenzie
Bailie Mrs Julia Fraser
Bailie John S. Maclean
Councillor Donald Gunn
Councillor Walter Lees

1944
Provost Alexander John Mackenzie
Bailie Walter Lees
Bailie William John Tolmie
Councillor Mrs Julia Fraser
Councillor Donald Gunn (Succeeded by Councillor Donald MacNeil)

1945
Provost Alexander John Mackenzie
Bailie William John Tolmie
Bailie John S. Maclean
Councillor Malcolm Maciver
Councillor John Morrison

1946
Provost Alexander John Mackenzie
Bailie John Kennedy
Bailie William John Tolmie
Councillor John Morrison
Councillor John M. Bain

1947
Provost Alexander John Mackenzie
Bailie John Kennedy
Bailie William John Tolmie
Councillor John Morrison
Councillor John M. Bain

1948
Provost Alexander John Mackenzie
Bailie John Kennedy
Bailie William John Tolmie
Councillor John M. Bain
Councillor Abraham Langley

1949
Provost Alexander John Mackenzie
Bailie John Kennedy
Bailie William John Tolmie
Councillor John M. Bain
Councillor Malcolm Smith

1950
Provost Alexander John Mackenzie
Bailie John Kennedy
Bailie John S. Maclean
Councillor John M. Bain
Councillor Malcolm Smith

1951
Provost Alexander John Mackenzie
Bailie John Kennedy
Bailie John S. Maclean
Councillor John M. Bain
Councillor Malcolm Smith

1952
Provost Alexander John Mackenzie
Bailie John M. Bain
Bailie Malcolm Smith
Councillor Donald J. Stewart
Councillor Rev. Canon H. Anderson Meadan

1953 (May)
Provost Alexander John Mackenzie
Bailie John M. Bain
Bailie Malcolm Smith
Councillor Donald J. Stewart
Councillor Abraham Langley

1953 (November)
Provost Alexander John Mackenzie
Bailie Malcolm Smith
Bailie Donald J. Stewart
Councillor Abraham Langley
Councillor Albert Nicoll

1954
Provost Alexander John Mackenzie
Bailie Malcolm Smith
Bailie Donald J. Stewart
Councillor Abraham Langley
Councillor Albert Nicoll

1955
Provost Alexander John Mackenzie
Bailie Dr Alexander Matheson
Bailie Donald J. Stewart
Councillor Abraham Langley
Councillor Albert Nicoll

APPENDICES

1956
Provost Alexander John Mackenzie
Bailie Dr Alexander Matheson
Bailie Donald J. Stewart
Councillor Abraham Langley
Councillor Albert Nicoll

1957
Provost Alexander John Mackenzie
Bailie Donald J. Stewart
Bailie Mrs Ann Urquhart
Councillor Abraham Langley
Councillor Albert Nicoll

1958
Provost Alexander John Mackenzie
Bailie Donald J. Stewart
Bailie Mrs Ann Urquhart
Councillor Donald Kenneth Maclean
Councillor Albert Nicoll

1959
Provost Donald J. Stewart
Bailie James Macrae
Bailie Mrs Ann Urquhart
Councillor Donald Kenneth Maclean
Councillor Albert Nicoll

1960
Provost Donald J. Stewart
Bailie Albert Nicoll
Bailie Mrs Ann Urquhart
Ex-Provost Alexander John Mackenzie
Councillor Abraham Langley

1961
Provost Donald J. Stewart
Bailie Albert Nicoll
Bailie Mrs Ann Urquhart
Ex-Provost Alexander John Mackenzie
Councillor Abraham Langley

1962
Provost Donald J. Stewart
Bailie Albert Nicoll
Bailie Mrs Ann Urquhart
Ex-Provost Alexander John Mackenzie
Councillor Abraham Langley

1963
Provost Donald J. Stewart
Bailie Albert Nicoll
Bailie Mrs Ann Urquhart
Ex-Provost Alexander John Mackenzie
Councillor Abraham Langley

1964
Provost Donald J. Stewart
Bailie John Macleod
Bailie Mrs Ann Urquhart
Ex-Provost Alexander John Mackenzie
Councillor Abraham Langley

1965
Provost Mrs Ann Urquhart
Bailie Donald Macleod
Bailie John Macleod
Ex-Provost Donald J. Stewart
Councillor Abraham Langley

APPENDICES

1966
Provost Mrs Ann Urquhart
Bailie John Macleod
Bailie James Macrae
Ex-Provost Donald J. Stewart
Councillor Abraham Langley

1967
Provost Mrs Ann Urquhart
Bailie John Macleod
Bailie James Macrae
Ex-Provost Donald J. Stewart
Councillor Alexander Matheson

1968
Provost Donald J. Stewart
Bailie James Macrae
Bailie Alexander Macdonald Matheson
Ex-Bailie John Macleod
Councillor Alexander Matheson

1969
Provost Donald J. Stewart
Bailie James Macrae
Bailie Alexander Macdonald Matheson
Ex-Bailie John Macleod
Councillor Alexander Matheson

1970 (May)
Provost Donald J. Stewart
Bailie James Macrae
Bailie Alexander Macdonald Matheson
Councillor Alexander Matheson
Councillor Donald Alexander Kennedy

1970 (November)
Provost Alexander Macdonald Matheson
Bailie James Macrae
Bailie Albert Nicoll
Councillor Donald Alexander Kennedy
Councillor Alexander Matheson

1971
Provost Alexander Matheson
Bailie James Macrae
Bailie Albert Nicoll
Police Judge John Macleod
Councillor Donald Alexander Kennedy

1972
Provost Alexander Matheson
Bailie James Macrae
Bailie Albert Nicoll
Police Judge John Macleod
Councillor Donald Alexander Kennedy

1973
Provost Alexander Matheson
Bailie James Macrae
Bailie Albert Nicoll
Councillor Murdo Macleod
Councillor Donald Alexander Kennedy

1974
Provost Alexander Matheson
Bailie James Macrae
Bailie Albert Nicoll
Councillor Murdo Macleod
Councillor Donald Alexander Kennedy

APPENDICES

1975
Provost Alexander Matheson
Bailie James Macrae
Bailie Albert Nicoll
Councillor Murdo Macleod
Councillor Donald Alexander Kennedy

30 May 1975
Passing of the Stornoway Trust Order and re-organisation of local government. Town Council members of the Trust relinquish office as Councillors.

Bibliography

Cameron, Ewen A., *Land For the People? The British Government and the Scottish Highlands, c.1880–1925*, Edinburgh, 1996

Cameron and Forrest Chartered Accountancy, 'Audit of Stornoway Trust 1924 to 1934', Inverness, 1935

Fresson, Edmund Ernest, *Air Road to the Isles*, Erskine, 1966

Haugh, Helen, 'Becoming Sustainable', Cambridge Judge Business School, 2021

Hunter, James, *The Making of the Crofting Community*, Edinburgh, 1976

Lawson, Bill, *Lewis in History and Legend: The East Coast*, Edinburgh, 2015

Leneman, Leah, *Fit for Heroes? Land settlement in Scotland after World War I*, Aberdeen, 1989

Lo Bao, Phil, and Hutchison, Iain, *BEAline to the Islands*, Erskine, 2002

MacDonald, Colin, *Life in the Highlands and Islands of Scotland: 'Echoes of the Glen' and 'Highland Journey'*, Moray, 1991

MacDonald, Donald, *Lewis: A History of the Island*, Edinburgh, 1990

MacRae, Kenneth A., *Diary of Kenneth A. MacRae: A Record of Fifty Years in the Christian Ministry*, Edinburgh, 1980

MacTV, *Arnish*, BBC Alba, 2022

Matheson, Sandy, 'Memoirs of the Western Isles Health Service', Western Isles Health Board, 2021, https://www.wihb.scot.nhs.uk/looking%20back/Stories/SandyMatheson.htm

Mòinteach gun Mhuileann, Moorland Without Turbines, 'The Case Against Turning Lewis into a Wind Power Station', 2004

Smith, Calum, *Around the Peat Fire*, Edinburgh, 2010

Sutherland, Halliday, *Hebridean Journey*, London, 1939

Wilson, John, *Tales and Travels of a School Inspector*, Edinburgh, 1928

Court of Session records

Hansard, *The Official Report of All Parliamentary Debates*, House of Commons

Official Reports, Scottish Parliament

Scottish Land Court records

The Scotsman, The Independent, Press and Journal, Stornoway Gazette, Northern Ensign, The Herald, West Highland Free Press

Index

Agricultural Executive
  Committee 90
Agriculture, Board of 45, 52,
  53, 84
  creation of new crofts on
    Lewis, wartime shelving of
    plans for (1914) 9–10
  'homes fit for heroes' pledge
    by Lloyd George, powers
    of compulsory purchase
    and 37–8
  land reform, Murray's call
    for 'strong and effective
    scheme', direction for 11–12
  land settlement programme
    after First World War,
    success (and problems) for
    33–4, 39, 40–1, 42–3
  raids by servicemen on dairy
    farms against proposals of
    (March 1919) 10
Aignish (township) 18

Air Ministry
  civilian flights, refusal of
    licence for 75–6
  Melbost golf links,
    appropriation for military
    purposes by 82
  Renfrew–Melbost air link
    permitted (inauguration,
    May 1944) 86–7
  Stornoway claimants seeking
    £35,000 compensation
    from 87
Air Road to the Isles (Fresson,
  E.E.) 62–3
Aird (township) 18
Aldred, Edwin (Stornoway
  Trust 'estate factor') 60–1,
  64, 73
  Carloway estate, ownership
    of 15
  golf club wartime reparations,
    help with 88–9

housing and social amenities, investigation of (1947) 94–5
land hunger recurrence in 1945, dealing with 84
long and faithful service (1928–61) 160
retirement of (1961) 103
Scottish Land Court, application for grazings at Steinish 65
Tolsta squatters, difficult relationship with 79–80
Allan, Alasdair, MSP 153, 155
Amalgamated Union of Engineering Workers (AUEW) 132, 133
Amec Foster Wheeler 142, 144–7, 148
Anderson, Lord Andrew 59
Anderson, Scottish Secretary William 23
Arnish (BBC Alba documentary, 1922) 126
'Arnish boots' (industrial footwear), vast sales of 127
Arnish moorlands 17
Arnish Peninsula 122
Arnish Point, Fred Olsen and development at 123–4, 125
Arnish workers
critical stoppage over 'safety measures ashore and afloat' (November 1979) 131–2
gold rush feeling for 127
industrial culture of 1970s, embrace of 127–8
stop-go, boom-and-bust nature of North Sea oil contracts, surprise at 126–7
Arnish yard
lease to team of former managers (1990) 134–5
roller-coaster career, continuation of (2020s) 158
Asquith, Herbert 34
Assynt Crofters Trust 162–3, 165
Assynt estate 162
Atlantic oil
concrete platforms for, benefits of 134
succession of Atlantic from North Sea oil 134
Atlee, Clement 89

Back (township) 18
Back Free Church 23
Bain, Provost John Louis 31, 58
Banks, Alasdair (planning officer) 152
Barvas estate 1, 14, 15, 144, 146
Barvas Estate Trust 167
Barvas Moor 18, 78
environment of global significance 150
wind farm on 142, 146–7, 150
Bayble (townships) 18

INDEX

Bays of Harris, working towards community ownership in 169
Benbecula, community ownership of 166–7
Bernera 30, 52
Bevan, Aneurin 113
BiFab yard at Methil 158
Birkenhead, Leverhulme's model village in 9
Black, Logan (Minch interconnector project manager) 157
Boundary Commission 151
BP Buchan Field 131
Branahuie (township) 18
Brand, Sheriff David 36
British Airways 87
British Energy 142, 144–7
British Railways 111
Broad Bay 17, 18
    land raids at (spring 1929) 47
Broker (township) 18
Burntisland Fabrications, Arnish yard and 158
Bute and Islay, fledgling air services to 64

Caithness and Sutherland Enterprise 162–3
Caledonian Hotel (Stornoway) 63, 67
Callanish 23
Cambrian Engineering 138, 139–40

Cambridge Judge Business School 95
Cameron, James (Inverness town clerk) 81–2
Cameron, Professor Ewen 46
Cameron and Forrest of Inverness (auditors) 59
Campbell, Angus (Comhairle nan Eilean Siar) 145–6
Campbell, Donald 24
Canadian Pacific 12, 24
Carloway estate 15
Carloway Estate Trust 169
climate change
    impact of fossil fuels and 140
    Kyoto Protocol to combat, adoption of (1997) 140–1
    wind power potential of Hebrides to combat 141
Climate Change Act (2008) 140–1
Cnoc Amhlaigh township 18
Cnoc nan Uan (Hill of the Lambs) 1
Coastal Command 75, 76
Coll (township) 18
Community Land Scotland 167, 168
Community Land Unit 165
community landownership in Scotland 53–4
    Bays of Harris, working towards community ownership in 169

Benbecula, community
    ownership of 166–7
Eriskay, community
    ownership of 166–7
Gigha, community ownership
    of 166
Great Bernera, working
    towards community
    ownership in 169
Knoydart, community
    ownership of 166
Stornoway Trust, community
    landownership for, reality
    of 54–5
West Harris, community
    ownership of 168–9
Western Isles, community
    ownership in, extent of
    (2017) 170
Congested Districts Board
    (Scotland) 33, 53
Congested Districts (Scotland)
    Commission 53–4
Cook, Bob (Assynt Crofters
    Trust director) 163
Court of Session in Edinburgh
    58–9, 60
Crawford, J.A. (advocate) 88
Creed salmon river 18
Crofters Commission 33, 36–7,
    71
Crofters Holdings (Scotland)
    Act 1886 5–6, 9, 33, 34
Crofting Commission 160–1

Cromore in Lochs 23

de Havilland *Dragon Rapide*
    biplane 62, 63, 86
Dingwall 13–14
Dodson, Councillor Keith 152
Douglas-Home, Alec 100–1
Drill Hall (Stornoway) 27, 28
Duncan, William (Maror Farm
    manager) 83

Eigg 164–5
  Isle of Eigg Heritage Trust
      165
  Runciman family on 164–5
Eisgean Estate 149
Eriskay, community ownership
    of 166–7
Ewing, Winifred 163

First World War 9–10
  memorial to fallen of,
      inauguration by Viscount
      Leverhulme of 1–3
*Fit for Heroes? Land Settlement
  in Scotland After World War I*
    (Leneman, L.) 37
Flesherin (township) 18
Fraser, Tom (Under-Secretary of
    State for Scotland) 89–91
Fred Olsen Ltd 122, 123, 130,
    133, 158
Free Church of Scotland 11, 20,
    23, 68, 82, 83, 124

INDEX

Fresson, Captain Ernest Edmund 'Ted' 62–3, 66–8, 75–6, 87
   Stornoway–Inverness exploratory flight by 67–8

Galloway, Ken (Stornoway Historical Society) 60
Galson estate 15, 30, 144, 146
Galson Estate Trust (Urras Oighreachd Ghabhsainn) 167
Garrabost (township) 18
General, Municipal, Boilermakers and Allied Trades Union (GMB) 136
General Election (1918) 27; (1923) 23; (1935) 74; (1970) 106; (2005) 151
Gigha, community ownership of 166
Gilchrist, Sir Andrew 122, 123
Gilmour, Sir John (Scottish Secretary) 48–9
Gladstone, William Ewart 5
Glasgow *Herald* 92
Glumaig Bay (Arnish) 123–4
Graauwmans, Henk 134, 136–7
Grazings Committees 147
Great Bernera, working towards community ownership in 169
Gress (township, and salmon river) 18

Harland and Wolff 158
Harris 6, 8, 13, 44, 50
   alcohol ban, lack of application on 20–1
   Bays of Harris, working towards community ownership in 169
   boundary between Lewis and, problem with 118–19
   death of Leverhulme, effects on 51–2
   new textile venture on, freight charges problem for 108–9
   North Harris Trust 166
   rehousing of people on, difficulty of 43
   renewable energy, investigation in north of 148
   Talla Na Marra in West Harris 168–9
   unrest on, resettlement problems and 12
Harris tweed 31–2, 101
   cyclical declines in industry 123
   Kenneth Mackenzie tweed mill 105
   rise of Stornoway's mills (1960s) 104
   self-employed weavers in industry, cruel problem for 107–8
Haugh, Professor Helen 57, 95–9

Hebridean Housing Partnership 168
Hebridean Journey (Sutherland, H.) 19
Hebrides
  'homes fit for heroes' pledge, radical implications for 38
  land raiding on, resumption of (1924) 23–4
  meritocracy and social mobility, Donald Stewart as example of 104–5
  National Registration Officer for 81–2
  parliamentary representation for, sea-change in (1975) 118–19
  restricted travel zone in wartime Britain 81–2
  safest area in wartime Britain 81
  'Spanish flu' pandemic (1918–20) in 25
Heerema Engineering Services 132–3, 133–4, 136
Highland Airways 62, 66–8
Highland Prospect Limited 163
Highland Regional Council 163
Highlands and Islands
  clearances, Murray's reference to 39
  creation of new crofts in 33–4
  land settlement, landowner intransigence on 36–7
  landlordism in, shifting edifices of 165
  nationalised estates in 53
  oil boom and construction, benefits for 128
Highlands and Islands Development Board (HIDB) 94, 108, 110
  wide-ranging and well-financed remit of 109
  Yukon comes to Lewis, HIDB and 121, 122, 128
Highlands and Islands Enterprise 163, 165
Hitler, Adolf 76, 87
Hunter, James 33–4, 37, 38
Hunter, Stewart (Lewis Offshore project manager) 132
Hurd and Schmidt consultancy (and 1947 report from) 94–5

The Independent 164
Inverness County Council 20–1, 120
HMY *Iolaire* tragedy off Stornoway (1 January 1919) 25

Jackson of Swordale, Major Randle 69–70
John Muir Trust 166
John R. Stutt of Paisley 89
Johnston, Tom MP 48

INDEX

Jones, Claire (Stornoway Wind Farm) 157

Kennedy, Charles 163
Kenneth Mackenzie tweed mill 105
Kishorn, construction yard at 128
Knock (township) 18
Knoydart, community ownership of 166

Lawson, Bill 45
Laxdale, housebuilding at (1945) 84
Laxdale salmon river 18
Lees, Bailie Walter 88
Leneman, Dr Leah 37, 43–4, 52
Leòdhasaich 9, 44, 87, 91, 124, 125, 134
   Celtic twilight, lingering attachment to 139
   familiarity with worldly ways 126
   'land reform' and, comparison with mainland agitation 103
   peat bogs, essential for 18
   workers from, sense of own agency among 130–1
Lever Brothers 4
   responsibilities in Hebrides for, Leverhulme's agreement on 51

Leverburgh 52
Leverhulme, Elizabeth Ellen Hulme, Lady 4
Leverhulme, William Hesketh Lever, Viscount 22, 25, 30, 32, 33, 100, 142, 170
   commercial realities of plan for Lewis, problems in 8–9
   crofting, antipathy towards 38
   death of (7 May 1925) 50
   division of Lewis, proposal for 13
   financial difficulties overseas, effect on (1921) 12
   honeymoon cruise to Scottish islands (1874) 4
   insensitivity of plans, autocratic delivery of 104
   lack of provision on future of holdings after death 51
   Lewis, plans for 7–8
   Lewis (and Stornoway) as plaything for 96–7
   Lewis estate, surrender of 13, 44–5
   Lewis people's 'love of home,' recognition of 5
   marketing opportunities, eye for 7
   'megalomaniac' accusation by Colin MacDonald of 10
   memorial to fallen, inauguration of (1924) 1–3

milk supply development plans 97–8
milk supply for Stornoway, problem for 48
offer from, improvement to encompass all old parish of Stornoway 16
opposition to plans, bunker effect on 12
ownership of Lewis estate, announcement of surrender of 13
plans for Lewis, mission to expand population 6–7
population imbalance, mission to correct 7
purchase of entire island of Lewis (1918) 4
rejection of proposal for division of Lewis (District Committee, 1923) 14–15
removal of Lewis from open market, 'homes fit for heroes' and 38
Stornoway following departure of, Sutherland's perception of 19
time for development of schemes, call from (Back district, 1919) 11
Trust Deeds, delivery to Stornoway of (January 1924) 18

'you have bought this island, but you have not bought us' (returned serviceman, 1919) 11
Lewis 9–10
alcohol ban on (1918) 20
boundary between Harris and, problem with 118–19
British Legion branch for 90
conditions in, worst since Hungry Forties in (1923) 23
crofting century (twentieth) on 46
death of Leverhulme, effects on 51–2
death of Leverhulme, recognition on 50–1
declining role within United Kingdom of 15
drinking dens on 22
emigration from, continuation of (1924) 23–4, 25
fishing industry, deep depression in (1923) 23
Free Church Presbytery of 68
Great War, death toll from 25
harvesting problems on (1923) 23
industrial world, Arnish Point and introduction to 126
'Isle of Lewis' model homes 93

land raids on, continuation of (spring 1929) 47–8
Minch interconnector to, Ofgem agreement for 157
Minch interconnector to, planning application for 147
Minch interconnector to, UK postponement of 155–6
MWT 'Case Against Turning Lewis into Wind Power Station' 144–51
National Health Service (NHS), impact on 112–17
Point peninsula on, crofting resettlement on Skye of people from 42–4
population contraction (1931–51) 86
population expansion on (1821–1931) 6
population of, haemorrhage of (1920s) 24–5
population reductions (1951–71) 107
population rise (2001–11) 158
potato crop, failure of (1923) 22–3
prohibition referendum (1921) 27
raids on farms throughout 1930s, land hunger and 79
Saudi Arabia of renewable energy, future as 141, 155
seaplane service to, proposal for 75
teetotalism on, rejection of 21
tourist industry on, niche nature of 129
women's suffrage movement, effect in 27
'Lewis and windfarms' (RSPB leaflet) 149, 150
Lewis Dairy Farmers Association Ltd (LDFA) 97, 98
Lewis District Committee 13, 14–15
  community landowners, risks for 53
  local government, sub-division of 119
Lewis District Council 150
Lewis Hospital (Goathill Road) 113–14
Lewis in History and Legend: The East Coast (Lawson, W.) 45
Lewis Island Preserved Specialities Company 60
Lewis Labour Party 74
Lewis Offshore Ltd 125, 129
  Atlantic oil and 134, 137
  boom-and-bust period for (1980s) 133
  BP Cleeton contract (£6 million) for 133

critical stoppage over 'safety
  measures ashore and afloat'
  (November 1979) 131–2
deunionisation of 133
Drillmaster rig, conversion of
  121, 132
ferry for South Uist–Eriskay
  route, *Eilean na h'Oige* 132
Fred Olsen pull-out from
  (1982) 132–3
Heerema Engineering in
  charge at (and sudden exit,
  1988) 133–4
Highland oil fabrication
  industry 'guerrilla' 137
island allowances, problem
  for 130
Lonka (steel barge), launch of
  (1977) 127, 130
management buyout 134–7
strikes at (late 1970s),
  popularity of 130–1
subcontractors, use of (and
  problems with) 127–8
Lewis Steam Laundry 54–5,
  97
Lewis Wind Power 142, 144–5
  extent and ambition of plans
  143–4
  perseverance of 156
  rejection of plans, bitter
  disappointment at 154
Lews Castle (Stornoway) 16,
  26, 50, 54
  Admiralty wartime
  requisition of 82
  Leverhulme's provisions for
  55–6, 58–9
  squatters in grounds (1950)
  84
  Victorian splendour of,
  purchase by Leverhulme
  (1918) 4–5
  'wasting asset' for Stornoway
  Trust 58–9, 60
Lews Castle College 125–6
  development as vocational
  polytechnic 101–2
Lews Castle Trust 56–7
Lionel School 22
Livingstone, Alexander
  MacKenzie, MP 23
Lloyd George, David 9, 10, 37–8
Local Government (Gaelic
  Names) (Scotland) Act
  (1997) 120
Lochs (parish) 1, 14, 16

Mac Fisheries 7
McAllister, Bill 133
Macaskill, Norman 134
Macaskill, Ossian 77, 78
Macaulay, Mary (later Mrs
  Kenneth Macmillan) 74
Macaulay, Murdo 28
Macdonald, Alex (Comhairle
  nan Eilean Siar) 145–6
MacDonald, Angus 135–6, 137

INDEX

MacDonald, Anne, Councillor 152
MacDonald, Calum, MP 143, 145, 147
   General Election (2005) for 151
   large-scale wind developments, support for 149
MacDonald, Colin (Board of Agriculture) 10, 52
Macdonald, D.J. (dentist) 115
MacDonald, Kenneth 77–8
McEwan, Provost Alexander of Inverness 105
MacEwen, Alexander 153
Macfarlane, Ian (AUEW Highland organiser) 132
MacFarquhar of Dell, Alexander 14
Macinnes, Reverend Donald John 51
MacIver, Colin 134
Maciver, Iain MacLennan 160–1, 162
MacIver, Kenny 129
MacIver, Murdo 134
Mackenzie, A.J. (Ross & Cromarty County Council) 90
Mackenzie, Provost Alexander John, 72, 84, 90
MacKenzie, Angus 28
Mackenzie, Colin Scott 78
Mackenzie, Donald G. 28
Mackenzie, Ebenezer 78
Mackenzie, Kenneth, Provost of Stornoway 3, 18, 21, 26, 31–2
   death of 76–7
Mackenzie, Molly 30
Mackenzie, Dr Murdoch, 29
Mackenzie, Norman 28, 30
Mackenzie, William 78
Maclean, Calum 105
MacLean, Murdo 28, 29–30
MacLennan, Catherine (Mrs Edwin Aldred) 60
Maclennan, Robert, MP 163
MacLennan, William (Lewis estate chamberlain) 70
MacLeod, Calum (Community Land Scotland) 168–9
Macleod, Donald (dairy owner on Scotland Street) 98
MacLeod, George 28, 78
Macleod, Hugh 30–1
MacLeod, Iain 161
MacLeod, John (returned serviceman) 11
MacLeod, Mary Anne 24
MacLeod of Dunvegan, Norman 42–3
Macmillan, Jessie 74
Macmillan, Kenneth 74
Macmillan, Malcolm K., MP 120, 153
   air transport links for Lewis, campaign for 73–5

family background 74
Nationalist challenges for (and unseating of, 1970) 105–6
re-election for Atlee's Labour Party (1945) 89
MacNeil, Angus Brendan, SNP winner in General Election (2005) 151
Macpherson, Sir Norman 88
Macquisten, Frederick Alexander, KC, MP
land reform and renewed land settlement, plea for 41–2
MacRae, James 31
MacRae, Reverend Kenneth A., wartime sabbath challenges for 82–3
MacTV 126
The Making of the Crofting Community (Hunter, J.) 33–4
Manor Farm moorlands 17
Mather, Jim, MSP and energy minister 154
Matheson, Alex (father of 'Sandy') 112, 113
practice of, Sandy's perspective on 114–15, 116–17
Matheson, Lieutenant-Colonel Duncan 4–5
Matheson, Mrs Alex (mother of 'Sandy') 115–16
Matheson, Provost Alexander ('Sandy') 111–12, 118, 119, 121
Amsterdam meeting with Heerema Engineering 133–4
economic development, vigorous attitude towards 120
genesis of 'biggest thing to hit Lewis' 122, 123–5
National Health Service (NHS), impact on Lewis 112–17
Sabbath question, oil developments and 124–5
Stornoway born with ethos for civic duty 112
youngest Provost of Burgh of Stornoway (until 1975) 118
Matheson, Sir James 5, 26, 96
Matheson family, landowners of Melbost 71
Melbost (township) 18
aerodrome at, land raids by returned servicemen at (1945) 84
appropriation for military operations 82
gateway for US Forces 82
Melbost Farm, land raids at (spring 1929) 47–8

INDEX

Melbost golf links 63, 66, 67
   crofting and golfing, uneasy relationship between 68–9, 71
Melbost machair, arrival of golf on 69
SS *Metagama* (emigrant ship) 12–13, 19, 24, 25, 30
Michie, Ray 163
Midland & Scottish Air Ferries Ltd 63–5
Mill Glen House 30
Mitchell Cotts, Sir William, MP 22
Moorland Without Turbines (MWT, Mòinteach gun Mhuileann) 144–51, 155
   industrialisation of landscape, windfarms and 145–7
   Lewis Wind Power rejection, pleasure in 154–5
   wind ranches, opposition to (rather than wind farms) 149–50
Morison, Thomas Brash, Solicitor-General for Scotland 40
SS *Morloch* (emigrant ship) 24, 25
Morrison, Alasdair, MSP 143, 153
Morrison, John MacRitchie 28, 29

Muirhead, Lieutenant-Colonel Anthony, MP 73–4
Mull, tourist industry on 128
Munro, Robert, Scottish Secretary of State 11, 12, 40, 42, 43
Murray, Dr Donald (later MP) 29, 74, 120
   enlistment from Lewis, 1918 speech to Parliament on sacrifice of 2
   land reform on Lewis, calls for 11–12
   land settlements, maiden speech on 38–40, 45
   Portnalong transplantation, awareness of 43
   Stornoway Golf Club, address to fellow golfers at 69
   working men, maiden parliamentary speech on livelihoods for 5–6

National Census (1921) 32
National Census (1931) 24–5
National Census (1951) 85–6
National Census (1981) 128
National Lottery 166
National Prohibition Act (Volstead Act, US) 20
Ness, crofting district of 13
   district Nursing Committee at 22

working bothan as public bar in 22
Ness–Tolsta road works 22
New Age philosophies 164
Nicolson Institute 27, 28, 50, 74, 143
North Assynt Estate 163
North Harris Trust 166
North Lochinver estate 162
North Lochs 17, 90
Northern Ensign 56
Novar, Viscount Ronald Munro Ferguson, Scottish Secretary 22

Obbe, townland of 52
Olsen, Fred 123, 124–5, 130, 136
Ontario Assisted Passages Scheme 24
Österle, Gotthilf Christian Eckhard ('Maruma') 164–5
Outer Islands Fishery Scheme 109

Pairc 15
Pairc Trust 167–8
Pier and Harbour Commission 105
Point peninsula ('Peninsula of Eye') 17–18
Port Sunlight 9
Portnaguran (township) 18
Portnalong (Skye) 53

fishing in lives of Lewis people at 43–4
transplantation of Rubhaich crofters and families to 43–4
tweed industry survival at 128
Portvoller (township) 18
prefabs, thriving subculture around 92–3
Press and Journal (Aberdeen) 64–5, 72, 131, 133, 135
Price, John (Amec Foster Wheeler) 145, 147
Pringle, Margaret 29
Pryde, John Monro 28

Ramsay, Thomas 74
Ranger, Samuel 31
Renfrew Airport 64
Representation of the People Act (1918) 27
Ross, Kenny 63, 67
Ross & Cromarty County Council 13–14, 21
pioneering council-house schemes, participation in (1930s) 91–2
Royal Air Force 76
RAF Dalcross, Inverness 86
wartime sabbath recognition by 82–3
Royal Commission on Local Government in Scotland 118

INDEX

Royal Flying Corps 62
Royal Society for the Protection of Birds (RSPB) 156–7
Rubhaich 18, 43, 53
Runrig 163

Salmond, Alex 163
Scandinavian Property Services Ltd 162
Schellenberg, Keith 164–5
Scotsman, The 58, 70–1, 79, 80
Scottish Airways 75
Scottish Crofters Union 160
   Assynt branch of 162
Scottish Department of Agriculture and Fisheries 168
Scottish Land Court 46–7, 71
   Stornoway claimants seeking £35,000 compensation from Air Ministry 87
   Stornoway Trust, application for landing field at Steinish to 65
Scottish Land Fund 166
Scottish Land Reform Act (2003) 166
Scottish Landowners Federation 167
Scottish National Party (SNP) 105, 143, 151, 153
Scottish Natural Heritage 163
Scottish Office 45

Scottish Parliament 152–3
   'green' energy programme for islands, SNP administration and 154
   Lewis Wind Power, decision against development by (April 2008) 154
Scottish Parliamentary Election (1999) 143
Scottish Parliamentary Election (2007) 153
Scottish Parliamentary Election (2011) 155
Scottish Trades Union Congress (STUC) 109–10
Scottish Transport Group 110
Second World War 75–6
   declaration of (3 September 1939) 81
   end in Europe of (May 1945) 83
   wartime losses, first war compared 85
Sheshader township 18
Shulishader township 18
Skye
   Borve and Annishadder estate in north of 163
   crofting developments on Raasay and (1919–27) 45
   crofting resettlement of Lewis people at Portnalong 42–3
   Cuillins of, attraction of 129

Glendale estate on 53–4
population contraction
(1931–51) 86
tourist industry on 128
Small Landholders (Scotland)
Act (1911) 34, 36
Smith, Angus 28, 30
Smith, Calum ('Safety') 24,
34–5, 78, 103
Smith, Donald Murdo ('D.M.')
159–61
  Amsterdam meeting with
Heerema Engineering
133–4
  genesis of 'biggest thing to hit
Lewis' 122
  raised in embrace of
Stornoway Trust 103
  Sabbath question, oil
developments and 124–5
Smith, Provost Roderick
('Roddy') 31, 92, 112
Smith's Shoe Shop (Cromwell
Street) 127
South Uist Estates (Stòras
Uibhist) 166–7
Soval 15
Statistical Account of Scotland
16–18
Steinish
  air landing strip at 64–6
  machair, arrival of golf on 69
Stewart, Charlie (at Bragar
meeting, April 2004) 146

Stewart, Donald James, MP
111–12, 120, 142–3, 153
  achievements (and
electability) of 105
  Hebridean meritocracy and
social mobility, example of
104–5
  Hebridean parliamentary
representation, spearhead
of sea-change in (1975)
118–19
  seventeen-year tenure as MP,
end of (1987) 142–3
  Stornoway Trust member
elected MP (1970) 106–7
  transport system on
Lewis, calls for major
improvements to 109–11
  Western Isles unemployment,
parliamentary debate on
(1971) 107–9
Stewart, Jessie Mary 104
Stewart, Neil (drift-net
fisherman) 104
Stornoway 1, 14
  air route to, pioneering on
62–5
  airport at, ups and downs of
development of 63–6, 68–9,
73, 75–6
  building trade in, serious
condition of 108
  endless renewal requirement
for 77

INDEX

English as language of business for 32
Free Church of Scotland in, wartime sabbath challenges for 82
Gaelic speakers in 32
gold rush feeling in, Arnish workers and 127
Harris tweed, rise of mills in (1960s) 104
Lewis Offshore and gold rush feeling in 127
United Free English Church in 51
Western Approaches, guardians of 82
Stornoway Fish Processing Company (and Fish Offal Works) 54–5
Stornoway Fish Products and Ice Company 60, 97
Stornoway Gas Company 54, 97, 98
Stornoway Gazette 35, 111–12, 119
Stornoway Golf Club 69–71
   aerodrome development, concerns about (1933) 73
   celebration of popularity and fundraising for (1913) 72–3
   construction of new 18-hole course for (1946–7) 89
   seeking compensation from Air Ministry for wartime land use 87
Stornoway Historical Society 60
Stornoway parish, extent of 16–18
Stornoway Town Council
   Arnish Point development, doubts about 124
   divided loyalties between Trust and Town Council members 91–2
   local government, sub-division of 119
   pioneering council-house schemes, participation in (1930s) 91–2
   powers inherited by Comhairle nan Eilean 120
   protest about insufficient council house building (1947) 94
   Stornoway Trust, negotiations for creation of 15–16
   Stornoway Trust, synergetic relationship with 120–1
Stornoway Trust 15, 18, 51, 97
   air travel to Stornoway, commitment to 63–6, 68–9, 73, 75
   appointments by (1928) 60
   approval by Town Council for creation of (November 1923) 16

Arnish Point development, commitment to 123–5
Arnish Point development, Fred Olsen's deal with 123–4, 125, 130–1
Arnish Point development, Sabbath question concerning 124–5
Assynt Crofters Trust and (no longer alone) 163
Baile Ùr Tholastaidh (New Tolsta), creation of settlement of 45
'Becoming Sustainable' report (2021) 95–9
Bhaltos crofting estate and 165–6
Cameron and Forrest audit for (June 1935) 59
candidates in first election (February 1924) 28
collaborative approach to development 100
common grazings, squatters on, problem for (1924) 46–7
as community landholder, reduction to only second-biggest (2007) 167
community landownership for, reality of 54–5
confident uniqueness of 160
contribution to national debate, D.M. Smith's perspective on 103–4
crisis responsibilities, recognition of (January 1924) 26
decennial anniversary elections (1934) 76–7
Deeds of Trust received from Leverhulme's solicitors (January 1924) 18
direct elections for four-year terms to (post-1975) 120–1
divided loyalties between Trust and Town Council members 91–2, 94
Eagleton, creation of new crofts at 45
elected chairs (1922–present) 171–2
electorate for, changes in (1994) 161
energetic activity in Lewis, reflection on 129
establishment of 26
estate factors over 100 years 160–1
estate policy, reactions to 144
factors (1924–present) 171
fiftieth anniversary year (1974), coming of age 125–6
financial problems for 55–6, 57–8
first election for members (February 1924) 27–30

INDEX

Fraser's post-war visit, land and housing of interest 89–91

Gress Farm, creation of new crofts at 45

Heads of Agreement with Amec/British Energy 146

HIDB approach on manufacturing development (early 1970s) 121

holdings enlarged by 276 new crofts (1919–27) 45

independence asserted, Melbost Farm and dairy needs of town 48–9

lack of guidance models for 52–3

land raids at Melbost by returned servicemen (1945), dealing with 84

land settlement schemes, Fraser's perspective on 90–1

landless cottars and squatters on estate of 34–6

lease of Arnish yard to team of former managers (1990) 134–5

Lewis peat bog, suggestions of exploitation of 150–1

Lewis Wind Power application, benefits for 152

Lews Castle, financial relief on Admiralty wartime requisition of 82

Lews Castle College, development of 101–2

Lews Castle 'wasting asset' for 58–9, 60

local needs, responsiveness to 129

Lord's Day preservation, air travel and 65

Macaulay Road housing scheme, ambition of 93–4

Manor Farm and 77

Manor Farm wartime sabbath challenge 83

Manor Park council-house scheme 91

member Donald Stewart elected MP (1970) 106–7

membership of (1924) 26

milk supply for Stornoway, problem for 48

nationalisation at local level, uniqueness as guide to 104

pioneering council-house schemes, participation in (1930s) 91–2

Plasterfield, land at 93

poaching incident at Glumaig Bay 157–8

post-war challenges facing (1946) 86–7

post-war housing problem for, dealing with 90–4
potential for wind power production on Lewis, exploitation of 141–2
profitability in fiscal year (1946–7), pride in 94
prospectus of (January 1924) 26
Provosts of Stornoway as chairs at (until 1981) 31
reconstruction of Stornoway town and employment creation projects (1947–60) 99
renewable energy plans, holding pattern for 155
renewables initiatives 139, 140, 141–2
Renfrew–Melbost air link permitted by Air Ministry (inauguration, May 1944) 86–7
rents and fuel-duties, main assets of 59–60
reparation claims for wartime annexations, process of 87–8
sales of properties by, prohibition without parliamentary approval 56
Scottish Land Court, application for landing field at Steinish to 65

social problems, almost endemic nature for 78
squatters, dealing with problem of 78–80
stability of Lewis, first task for 19
stable, profitable and responsible social landowner 99
stewardship of 1,307 crofts inherited by 44–5
stop-go, boom-and-bust nature of North Sea oil contracts, surprise at 126–7
Stornoway Town Council, synergetic relationship with 120
territory of 53–4
tourism and social amenity provision, looking forward on 95
trustees elected to (1924–2018) 172–9
Upper Coll Farm, creation of new crofts at 45
war drums over Europe (1937) and 80–1
wind-farming, excursion into large-scale farming in Lewis 138–9
wind power proposal on land of, approval of 156–7
Stornoway Trustees 18
Stornoway Wind Farm 156–7

INDEX

Sutherland, Dr Halliday 19–20, 21, 52
Sutherland, Liz 43–4
Swordale (township) 18

Talla Na Marra (West Harris) 168–9
Tarbert 166
Temperance (Scotland) Act (1913) 20
Third Reich, defeat of 76
Times, The 4
Tolmie, Bailie W.J. 80–81
Tolmie, David 29
Tolmie, Dr John 76–7
Tolmie, John Pringle 28, 29
Tolsta (townships) 17, 18
   registered crofters and squatters in, friction between (1935) 79–80
Tong (township) 18, 34
Toothill, Sir John 111
Tourism in Scotland, Potential Impact of Wind Turbines on (VisitScotland report) 148
Traigh Mhor (Barra), exploratory air landing at 64
Trump, Donald John 24
Trump, Fred 24

Uig 1, 13, 14, 16, 30
United Nations (UN)
   Kyoto Protocol 140–1, 145
   Ramsar Convention 150
Upper Coll township 18
Urquhart, Provost Ann 121

Vatisker (township) 18
Vestey, Edmund 162
Volstead, Andrew 20

Walker, David 134
War Office 81–2
Webster, Peter 134–6, 137
West Harris, community ownership of 168–9
West Highland Free Press 149
Western Isles (Na h-Eileanan an Iar) 151
   autocratic private landlordism dead and buried in 170
   community ownership in, extent of (2017) 170
Western Isles Council (Comhairle nan Eilean) 93, 160
   achievements of, impressive nature of 120
   wind fund 147
Western Isles Council (Comhairle nan Eilean Siar, post-1997) 141
   boundaries of 120
   Lewis Wind Power planning permission debate 152
   Stornoway Wind Farm approval 157

Western Isles Health Board 112, 117
Wheatley, Lord John (and Wheatley Commission) 118–19
Wheatley proposals, Joint Advisory Committee on 119–20
Wilson, Brian, MP 138, 145, 165